D0745797

ALSO BY ADRIAN GOSTICK AND CHESTER ELTON

All In

The Carrot Principle

What Motivates Me

THE

BEST TEAM WINS

THE NEW SCIENCE OF HIGH PERFORMANCE

ADRIAN GOSTICK AND **CHESTER ELTON**

SIMON & SCHUSTER PAPERBACKS

NEW YORK   LONDON   TORONTO   SYDNEY   NEW DELHI

Simon & Schuster Paperbacks
An Imprint of Simon & Schuster, Inc.
1230 Avenue of the Americas
New York, NY 10020

This Simon & Schuster paperback export edition February 2018

SIMON & SCHUSTER PAPERBACKS and colophon are registered
trademarks of Simon & Schuster, Inc.

For information about special discounts for bulk purchases,
please contact Simon & Schuster Special Sales at
1-866-506-1949 or business@simonandschuster.com.

The Simon & Schuster Speakers Bureau can bring authors to your live event.
For more information or to book an event, contact the
Simon & Schuster Speakers Bureau at 1-866-248-3049
or visit our website at www.simonspeakers.com.

Interior design by Ruth Lee-Mui

Manufactured in the United States of America

10   9   8   7   6   5   4   3   2   1

ISBN 978-1-5011-9184-8
ISBN 978-1-5011-7987-7 (ebook)

CONTENTS

SOLVING THE MODERN PROBLEMS OF TEAMWORK

What Today's Best Managers Are Doing Differently

Chris Hadfield looks like a fireman, or maybe a high-school biology teacher. He's neither. The trim, mustachioed Canadian is an astronaut and a member of a select group of only two hundred people who have walked in space. *Forbes* has called him the most famous astronaut since Neil Armstrong. During his five-month stint as commander on the International Space Station, he was certainly the most social-media savvy. Hadfield gave up the first few hours of shut-eye each night so he could float around sending messages via Facebook and Twitter about stuff that most astronauts take for granted but the rest of us find fascinating, like how to make a sandwich in microgravity, how to get your hair cut, or how to wring out a washcloth.

Millions watched Hadfield's messages, and he did more to generate public interest in space travel than anyone for decades. But his greatest contribution may not be in his tweets and posts, but in the way he led his diverse team. He told us that before he assumed his role as commander, he knew the mission would be a management challenge. His team was comprised of smart, driven Americans and Russians—the oldest and youngest two and a half decades apart in age. Not only might generational divides develop, but language barriers and cultural misunderstandings could create issues. And here was a young man from Sarnia, Ontario—who looks a lot like an after-school driving instructor—and he was about to tell them what to do twenty-four hours a day.

So, before they even thought about strapping themselves into their rocket, Hadfield got to know his people. He taught himself Russian. He moved to the United States for a time, and then to Russia, where he didn't live in a hotel but in state housing. Then, he brought his team together to learn how they could respect each other and work best together. The six met each other's families, heard everyone's back stories, ate Big Macs, and downed a little vodka. Hadfield even had them role play how they would support each other if one of them lost a loved one while in space, which, remarkably, did happen to one of the astronauts during their mission. Hadfield's goal: By the time they rocketed out of orbit, he wanted them to not just be coworkers but a codified, unified team.

Their mission was wildly successful from a scientific and public relations perspective; but more remarkably, during their five months in space, Hadfield told us his team members never had a single heated argument. Not one. They worked together beautifully.

We all know how hard it can be to get our stressed out, spread thin modern teams to work together when they can go home after eight or nine hours, let alone when they're "[S]itting in a tin can far above the world." *The new kid isn't pulling his weight. Ruth isn't responding to my texts. Does Sarah have to send an email about everything? Steve is focused on the wrong stuff!* What team leader isn't hearing such gripes, or others? Hadfield's multigenerational, global team eschewed such bickering and operated in harmony because he understood how certain soft skills can help build today's best teams. By using his considerable leadership talents, he came up with resourceful ways of creating bonds of understanding among his team members that went well beyond the standard rule book for running the station.

In space, he explained to us, there are lots of written rules: There are books *full* of them. They are important because when you don't follow procedures, things can go wrong and everyone could, well, die. Usually the margin of error is a few seconds. In the opening scene of the movie *Gravity*, an astronaut, played by actress Sandra Bullock, disobeys mission control and her leader (actor George Clooney) for just a moment. Hadfield told us that would never happen in real life. Astronauts always follow the rules. They are sacrosanct. Yet Hadfield's team was equally committed to one *unwritten* rule, which they collectively came up with, that became just as important as the formal ones: Each member of the crew had to do one unsolicited kind thing for every other member of the crew every single day—for five months.

Hadfield said these random acts of kindness were often anonymous. One astronaut might help cook a meal when it wasn't his turn, another might tidy up a sleeping area for a crewmate who had to rush to duty, another might check a piece of support equipment or clean a filter for a team member who needed to get some rest. These actions focused each person on serving others, versus themselves, and kept tempers in check and egos in the right place. This one simple practice had a profound effect; Hadfield, in fact, credits it as being *the* most impactful in bringing his team together.

EVIDENCE OF PAYOFFS

Now, more than ever, businesses need great team leaders like Chris Hadfield, those with strong team leadership skills. The current era of unprecedented change in business has been described with another acronym to add to our lexicon: VUCA (pronounced *voo-ka*), which stands for volatility, uncertainty, complexity, and ambiguity. And one of the ways in which organizations are seeking to meet the challenges of a VUCA world is by making more work team-based. In fact, if you haven't noticed, we are smack-dab amid a massive shift toward more collaboration. Already, in the average company, up to 80 percent of employees' days are spent working in teams and, in a Deloitte survey of 7,000 senior executives in 130 countries, almost half said their companies were either in the middle of restructuring, or about to embark on it, to put more emphasis on teamwork.

The vogue for teams is driven by evidence for potential payoffs in higher-quality and faster problem-solving, which includes a fascinating study from professors at the University of Central Florida and a research psychologist with the U.S. Army that found the most effective teams have a collective intelligence that allows them to get more work done and spot problems quicker. We've also found that when people feel they are part of a collaborative, communicating work group they are overall happier on the job, which tends to make people more productive and efficient. All good stuff. Stanford and University of Michigan professors also have shown those in positive team environments have fewer accidents and health care costs 50 percent lower than those of their peers who are not in great teams.

Another payoff: The diversity of knowledge and experience that good teams bring to assignments allows them to be more responsive to customers—especially those of different ages and cultures for instance. And it's well documented that team collaboration spurs greater creativity and therefore more rapid innovation for customers, which is vital in today's ultra-competitive and rapidly evolving business environment. The need to develop more smart products, for example, which capitalize on the potential of new technologies, is requiring increased collaboration across departments—work that is best achieved by cross-functional teams.

One last payoff: Organizations are relying increasingly on teams because they allow for decentralized decision-making and speedier action, due to fewer layers of bureaucracy. So that means we are increasingly evolving from the outmoded command-and-control hierarchy to a network-of-teams approach, which, as General Stanley McChrystal wrote in *Team of Teams*, enables organizational flexibility, such as moving talent more seamlessly between work groups.

These benefits all sound pretty good, right? The problem is that most of the teams we find are nowhere near as effective as they could be, and worse, are often riven by massive tensions if not outright dissension. You might have been part of a dysfunctional team. Heck, every team can have stretches where things don't click. Such dysfunction drains employee energy, enthusiasm, and creativity rather than fueling them. A recent workplace survey by Salesforce.com shows a whopping 96 percent of executives cite poor collaboration and communication as the main sources of workplace failures, and only 14 percent of leaders (according to a Deloitte/Facebook study) are completely satisfied with their ability to collaborate and make decisions as teams. Ouch.

It might be the most pressing question businesses must address: How can managers better lead their teams to improved performance given all the distractions and challenges we face?

Here is where our findings come in. Considerable research into the factors driving the success of today's high-performance work teams shows that a set of disciplines makes the biggest difference. This research includes a number of recent high-profile reports as well as our own substantial study of team leadership.

THE SOFT STUFF IS THE HARD STUFF

A few years ago, Google conducted a prominent research study on teams called Project Aristotle. The company assembled some of its best statisticians and organizational psychologists to investigate why some of its work groups were more innovative and productive than others. It's a great question and, after half a decade of analysis, having evaluated more than 250 attributes of 180 teams at the company, the researchers concluded that the key factors in the superior performance of the best teams were not that they had more talented people or better technology or a better mix of skills; nor did they find that the best teams were more incentivized or led by more experienced managers. No, the five factors the researchers identified were goose-down soft. Team members in the best teams: Felt *psychologically safe* with one another, which meant they felt comfortable being vulnerable in the group and taking risks such as sharing an idea that might be perceived as wacky elsewhere; Felt that their fellow team members were *dependable*, in other words they trusted one another; Were clear about team *structure* and had *clarity* of plans and goals; Felt their work had personal *meaning*; and Believed their work would have a positive *impact* in the world.

Google's findings are backed up by more research. Another study, conducted by researchers at MIT and Union College, analyzed 192 teams and found that those with the highest collective intelligence and competence—measured by how the teams performed on a number of widely ranging tasks—had greater social sensitivity. In particular, the PhDs found, members were more *empathetic* about what others on the team were thinking and feeling.

The effective use of soft disciplines, "makes people feel valued and rewarded, gives them a clearer sense of high standards, and helps them feel more motivated," said Rick Lash, Hay Group's director for leadership and talent. The management consultancy found managers who incorporate the soft side into their leadership approach can increase their team's performance by as much as 30 percent. The value of these skills was also highlighted by a large study of the U.S. labor market by Harvard economist David Deming, who found that wage growth—as measured across all sectors—has been considerably stronger in occupations where workers can develop strong soft skills to complement their analytical abilities. That means employers have placed a premium on those who can bring the soft with the hard.

We back this up with a bit of research of our own. A 300,000 person study by Willis Towers Watson for our book *All In* found high-performing managers excel at a group of key soft skills including inculcating a clear mission, developing more agility in their team members, sharing information transparently, and recognizing individual and team accomplishments. The use of these soft skills was correlated with workgroups that have stronger levels of employee engagement, as well as significantly higher customer satisfaction scores and team profitability. Not too shabby.

We could go on with the proof. We won't. In short, the case for the decisive role of soft skills in driving today's best teams has been won. The problem is that for most managers, the soft stuff is the hard stuff. We work with leaders of teams of all sizes—from those in small businesses to large multinationals—and most tell us that the people management side of their work is by far the most difficult aspect of their jobs. It is hard to lead a team and, despite all the advances we are making with digital tools and leadership science, it's getting harder still.

Almost every week, we speak to busy managers who are facing increasingly pressing trials that the most popular books on teamwork simply don't address. Just about every leader we meet has described some variation on these modern challenges of team leadership:

THE RISE OF THE MILLENNIALS. Younger employees, as a group, want to work and be managed in different ways from older team members, and from the ways most team leaders learned to manage. In this book, we are going to introduce you to findings from our 50,000 person motivation research database, which shows a clear preponderance of younger employees *prefer* to work collaboratively, which is good news as our traditional workplaces evolve into team structures. The challenges we find, however, are that they want much more coaching and feedback, and have a considerably stronger desire for *appreciation* of their work from their supervisors than older workers. They are also hopping from job-to-job much faster. Boomers' average tenure in their jobs is seven years, Gen Xers average five years per job, while Millennials are staying only one-and-a-half to two years on average. (Most of us have underwear we've hung on to longer than that.) Younger workers, therefore, not only are demanding a different style of management, they are creating more instability in teams. This requires leaders to ensure that their groups produce a smooth flow of work despite an almost constant ebb and flow of talent.

INCREASING SPEED OF CHANGE. Businesses of all kinds are evolving more rapidly due to fast-paced technological changes and the pressure to bring innovations to market faster. This means teams must be more agile and their make-up more fluid, with staff moved around as market- or customer-needs morph. As Cisco CEO John Chambers said, "Today we compete against market transitions not competitors. Product transitions used to take five or seven years; now they take one or two." Thus, getting people up to speed faster is a necessity, not a nice-to-have. And this means that today's team leaders are faced with the uphill task of training people quicker and helping them understand their roles in a fraction of the time allowed in the past.

MORE TEAMS WITH GLOBAL, VIRTUAL, AND FREELANCE WORKERS. With so much business now conducted globally—and with so many more remote and gig employees—many teams are often comprised of individuals spread out across the planet who rarely meet in person. Consider that 37 percent of employees now work virtually—whether from a remote location or their homes—and 93 percent of companies say they are regularly teaming freelancers up with full-time employees to work on projects. Today's work environments can also comprise workers from different cultures, with diverse working styles, and sometimes dissimilar perspectives about the right approach for getting the job done. Of course, these workers may also prefer different styles of management. The ability to manage without borders is becoming increasing critical for team leaders, yet it's never been more difficult to create a sense of common team culture, make every worker feel connected and integral to the group, and facilitate clear, inclusive, and frequent communication among members.

CROSS-FUNCTIONAL FRICTION. We have yet to meet a leader who doesn't want to build bridges within his or her organization and break down silos. It is certainly in fashion to bring together cross-functional teams to develop more creative and inclusive product development and service delivery. The downside is that many of these teams end up being hugely ineffective. Stanford University researchers found that three-quarters of cross-functional teams can be classified as dysfunctional. Despite the many ways companies have tried to facilitate collaboration across departmental lines, a 2016 study from the Hay Group revealed close to half of employees say their teams are still not adequately supported by other areas of the business. It's as if the Hatfields and McCoys are at work, with team members from different functional areas engaging in turf wars, unreceptive to input about how to do their work from those elsewhere, lacking appreciation for the challenges of others, and failing to understand the important mission of tasks completed in other teams.

LEADING TEAMS IN AN ERA OF UNPRECEDENTED CHANGE

Organizations have tried to solve these modern problems of teamwork in various ways. They've provided managers with better connectivity and collaboration technologies. Many teams now use virtual project management tools, shared calendars, internal chat systems, brainstorming and collaboration tools, employee engagement analytics platforms, and learning management systems. While this book is not about these tools, they certainly can increase efficiency. But a core finding is this: Tools alone cannot improve the quality of team-management.

Another common practice aimed at enhancing teamwork has been the systematic and widespread tearing down of physical walls dividing employees to build cooperative working environments. About 70 percent of offices are now open space, in theory, to get people talking, meeting more, and sharing ideas. Again, there's nothing wrong with this concept. But alone it does not stimulate genuine teamwork.

More extreme efforts to fundamentally restructure organizations have also been tried. Online shoe retailer Zappos has experimented with a flatter organization and self-management, through a structure CEO Tony Hsieh refers to as holacracy, in which traditional top-down reporting lines have been replaced by work circles that do not have traditional managers. In place, they appointed lead links, nominal managers with little formal authority. As might be expected, the system has presented some challenges, and interestingly, Zappos dropped off the *Fortune* Best Places to Work list for the first time in eight years after implementing the approach.

The bottom line is that no matter what experiments an organization conducts with operating structure, sophisticated collaboration tools, or physical environment, there is no skirting the fact that a manager's *soft* skills are vital in driving high performance and real teamwork.

Our task in this book is to help leaders understand how to effectively manage teams of people in this era of unprecedented change. We set out to find the answers, drawing on a wealth of studies, both our own and those of others, looking for the most scientifically grounded answers we could find. The research we tapped includes several of our own surveys of more than 850,000 people, data that helped us identify the traits of managers of the most successful teams and isolate disciplines of management that employees indicate are most motivating.

In addition, as of the end of 2017, more than 50,000 working adults, of all ages and from all around the world, had completed our Motivators Assessment. This is a 100 question scientific test to determine the features of work—including what style of management—most strongly motivates the person taking the assessment. The people who completed the test work in small businesses with fewer than ten people, all the way up to huge organizations with hundreds of thousands of employees. They work in all sectors, from information technology, to medicine, hospitality, nonprofits, K-12 and higher education, pharmaceuticals, energy, manufacturing, mining, media, banking, dining, consumer lending, advisory services, construction, telecommunications, government/public sector, and more. We found some striking patterns in their answers that provide strong support for the importance of the particular leadership methods we'll outline.

We also hit the road. We conducted site visits and interviews with a host of team leaders and employees in high-engagement, high-performance organizations around the world. We think those visits and interviews provide rich insights into how specific managers, like astronaut Chris Hadfield, implement a key set of practices we have found to be the most impactful on performance. The stories we will tell allow us to bring those practices to life through accounts of modern team leaders in action—from CEOs of major corporations to entrepreneurs with a handful of employees (meaning that you don't have to be big to benefit from these ideas). As one example, we'll explain how sales team leaders for the basketball team with the worst record in the NBA more than quadrupled season-ticket sales and set numerous league records by focusing on *hustle* instead of sales. We'll tell you how managers at one science and technology company found a way to get new team members up to speed faster by keeping them from doing their work for a full three months. And we'll show how one leader at an eighty-year-old helicopter manufacturer has created some of the most innovative creations in the sky by teaming up Hollywood sci-fi artists with his aerospace engineers.

Though we are sticklers about basing our recommendations on hard data, we are also strong believers in using the stories of real managers in action. Their examples populate the chapters to come, and we hope you enjoy meeting them.

We are also sensitive about how busy you are. As such, we will attempt to offer concise solutions, not complex or time-consuming advice. We have boiled down our findings about what works for high-performance team leaders into five practices that every manager can implement, starting tomorrow.

THE FIVE DISCIPLINES OF TEAM LEADERS

From the research and our hands-on work with teams around the world, we have identified this set of distinguishing characteristics of the management styles of the best leaders in modern teams:

Discipline 1: Understand Generations—
Help Millennials, Gen Xers, and Boomers Get Along

It's time to accept that we are different, after all. The best managers have learned to adapt to meet the special demands of Millennial employees, and have developed ways to cater better to their needs while creating stronger bonds between all generations. Our research has found a handful of stark differences in what motivates many Millennials in comparison to their older colleagues—some of which bucks conventional leadership wisdom. Perhaps most striking is the finding that while autonomy is one of the stronger motivators for Boomers and Gen X workers, it ranks near the bottom for Millennials. Another striking data point with Millennials is that recognition from their bosses and coworkers matters much more than it does to older workers. While these differences can cause considerable friction between young employees and their managers and older colleagues, we will show that they, in fact, can provide a basis for creating stronger bonds between the generations and to their organization.

Discipline 2: Manage to the One—Give the Man His Guitar

Lack of career development has become the number one reason why employees leave organizations—a change from just a few years ago when pay topped the list. The good news: Focusing on career development is a relatively low-cost way to keep people and keep them engaged, and is something well within the control of a manager. We will introduce our findings showing the considerable payoffs in increased commitment, creativity, and ultimately productivity, when leaders take even a small amount of time to personalize responsibilities based on team members' individual drivers. In most high-engagement teams, we discovered variations on a practice we call *job sculpting*, in which managers give each employee some work to do that is especially motivating to him/her, while altering or transferring other work that might be demotivating (if at all possible).

Discipline 3: Speed Productivity—
Help New People and Teams Work Faster and Smarter

The fluid composition of teams today and the rapid movement of people between jobs requires managers get new team members up to full productivity in a fraction of the time than even a few years ago. We introduce specific methods we've seen in action for the rapid integration of new people and entire teams, and outline the three-step process managers can use to build security, context, and affiliation.

Discipline 4: Challenge Everything—
Inspire Innovation Through Healthy Discord

Feeling comfortable to express one's views, take smart risks, and being given roughly equal time to speak up are the hallmarks of

psychological safety. Research shows that fostering these characteristics is vital for effective problem-solving and innovative thinking within a fast-moving team. We'll also introduce you to what
we call *the radical effect*—the remarkable payoff of having at least
one team member who regularly challenges assumptions and approach. But keeping debate from escalating into dissension and
backstabbing, while assuring that all team members get a roughly
equal hearing, is a tricky challenge; thus, we'll introduce the methods used by great team leaders to promote healthy discord.

Discipline 5: Now, Don't Forget Your Customers— Create Alignment Around Serving Them

In the most global, diverse, technologically driven workplace
in history, any manager who doesn't find time to understand
how to work more collaboratively with other functional areas is
going to be left behind. But we find the focus of all team efforts
must be kept rigorously on customers, whatever they look like.
With that as a foundation, turf consciousness begins to diminish
and purpose is much more clear.

Are there payoffs to all this discipline?

The results from better team leadership are profound. Consider that researchers at Gallup have found manager behaviors
explain 70 percent of the variance in employees' daily work engagement, and academics from Stanford University and the University of Utah have discovered that nine-person teams led by
engaging bosses are as productive as ten-person teams led by average or poor bosses. Our 300,000 person research study for *All
In* found profitability was as much as three times higher in work

groups where managers drove higher levels of worker engagement, enablement, and energy.

The vital role of the team leader became clear to us when we were having a conversation not long ago with Gerard Johan "G.J." Hart, CEO of California Pizza Kitchen. CPK is one of the top three companies in U.S. casual dining for comps—same-stores sales in comparison to previous year's—and achieves this with no major media advertising. Hart told us his company's success has come by building great team cultures—one at a time. "So goes the leader, so goes the rest," he said. "When I speak with my team leaders, I talk about the responsibility of developing and caring for the people they lead. We foster a culture in our industry of promoting operators from within; while they are great at the skills of running a restaurant, they might not have significant experience in developing and leading people. It doesn't matter if you graduated from Harvard or kindergarten, people follow you if you care for them and you are genuine."

To that end, Hart asks his team leaders to think of themselves as 911 operators. "When you call 911, you get someone who cares," he said. "You know they will resolve your issue and get you the help you need. That's what our managers have do for their people—be responsive and care."

At Tesco, the United Kingdom's largest grocery store chain, with 425,000 employees, Mark Chapman is the customer fulfillment director. Chapman made us smile with the following true account of a young store manager in his organization: "He was good with numbers and was brilliant about giving the perception of being a great leader, but I just had this nagging feeling he wasn't all he said he was. I asked him one day, 'Who's the most important person in your store?' With no pause, he said it was him. I asked, 'Why not the customer or your employees?' He said, 'Because I'm responsible for sales, the shrink, the wages.'"

So, Chapman gave the store manager an assignment. The next day he was to take all the store's cleaners—the people who mopped floors, polished registers, and emptied the dust bins—and put them on a minibus and take them to another store. The manager was to work with them all day as they cleaned.

The store manager laughed, but Chapman said he was serious. No joke. Moreover, he said, at the end of the day he wanted the bus to take each cleaner to his or her home and the store manager was to thank them personally as they got off.

The young man did as requested. Chapman said, "The next week I asked that manager, 'Who is the most important person in your store?' He said, 'The cleaners!'"

Now, Chapman's goal wasn't to convince this store leader that cleaners are more important than a general manager, but that everyone on his team must feel valued and appreciated—from the people pushing brooms to those ringing up customer orders, from the folks stocking shelves to those balancing the accounts.

Just think of the difference you feel when you are part of a vibrant team with a caring, attentive leader, someone who makes you feel included, trusted, and valued. And, on the flip side, who hasn't seen the corrosive effects of mediocre bosses? (Not to mention the influence of truly terrible bosses.)

If you are still not convinced, we hope you will be by the end of this book. Many of today's best organizations have come to understand how important changing their team leadership styles is in achieving great results. Consider what happened at Caterpillar, the $47 billion heavy equipment manufacturer and one of the world's most respected brands. After enhancing managers' soft disciplines in just one location, they found performance in that team had jumped by an astounding 70 percent; customer satisfaction by 34 percent; and absenteeism, turnover, and overtime dropped too—yielding an $8.8 million annual savings. No dummies, Caterpillar leaders then made this a management priority across its entire tough-as-nails organization. Wouldn't you? Today, the company has found that its best team leaders run business units that meet or exceed performance goals 40 percent more often than other units.

As you'll see, it is possible to lead your team to major improvements as well, no matter what you are seeking to achieve.

All it takes is a little discipline.

PART I

THE FIVE DISCIPLINES OF TEAM LEADERS

ONE

UNDERSTAND GENERATIONS

How to Engage Millennials, Gen Xers, and Boomers

Joan Kuhl describes herself as the Millennial Matchmaker. She runs the consultancy Why Millennials Matter and advises employers, including Goldman Sachs, Bristol-Myers Squibb, and Eli Lilly, on hiring and retaining recent college graduates. She believes that while managing Millennials presents a few distinctive challenges—for instance, many see nothing wrong with oversharing information about their lives (and work lives) on social media—there are also tons of positives. "We tend to publicize the outrageous acts of defiance," she says of the newest generation, but adds "the majority that I work with are very mission-focused and value-based."

Yet even this fan of the younger generation does grin when she thinks about some of the behavior of young people in her own office. She recalls one intern who ate a tuna-fish sandwich during a morning meeting with senior colleagues. When mildly rebuked after, the intern replied, "Well, you said to be myself, and I was hungry."

So much has been written about this Millennial generation (also known as Gen Y). They are supposedly narcissistic, lazy, entitled; constantly Snapchatting or Tweeting with the person in the next cubical. They don't respect authority, but want hand-holding and praise. And they're ready to skip off to a new job in a heartbeat. A *Time* magazine cover story called them the "Me, Me, Me Generation."

Our intention is not to bad-mouth Millennials. We personally think this generation has the creativity, drive, and technological aptitude to revolutionize our workplaces, and they absolutely *should* feel valued and rewarded for their contributions. Also note that we understand generalizations about generations always overstate differences, leading to grossly exaggerated caricatures. That's not our intent either. There is, of course, no such thing as a typical Millennial, Boomer, Gen Xer, or even the soon-to-emerge Gen Z. The definitions of when each generation begins and ends aren't even universally agreed upon. History doesn't punctuate so neatly for us. For our purposes, we'll accept these as the most commonly accepted delineations: Boomers were born between 1946 and 1964; Gen Xers between 1965 and 1984. As for Millennials, two of the leading authorities on generations, researchers Neil Howe and William Strauss, authors of *Generations: The History of America's Future*, say the last Millennial was born in 2004—and anyone coming thereafter will be Gen Z. You can find other dates to end the Millennials—from the mid-1990s on—with some saying Gen Z (or iGeneration) is already in the workplace in force. But Howe and Strauss are widely regarded as *the* experts on generations and we won't argue with them. So that means new workers entering the job market will be Millennials for a while longer (unless your new IT director is twelve years old).

With that said, while Millennials may have been unfairly caricatured, like generations before them, they do demonstrate some strong commonalities. Many of these are unique strengths we have not seen before, while others are presenting serious challenges to managers. And the worst thing we can do is ignore the differences.

THE NEED FOR BETTER PRACTICES

Why should we care about all of this? Why do we have to learn how to manage Millennials any differently? The first big reason: We've reached a tipping point. Millennials have edged out Boomers and Gen X as the largest generation at work; and by 2020, more than half of working adults worldwide will be Millennials. Consider your own team: Is it a homogenized cluster of similar-thinking, similar-looking, similarly aged folks with identical backgrounds and biases, or is it a collection of diverse people—some older, some younger—who come at work from different perspectives. And of your young workers, have you noticed a few differences? Scott Harner has.

Harner is team manager of Chip Ganassi Racing, which runs successful cars in NASCAR, the IndyCar Series, SportsCar Championship, and World Endurance Championship. His organization has teams of mechanics who keep cars running on the tracks, and noted that many Millennials bring an affinity for technology that is vital in racing today, but he's also seen a change in the work ethic in some of the young guys he hires. "This is hard work—twelve-hour days turning around a car that's crashed then jumping on a plane for another city. And we do it for six months in a row. A lot of the young guys flame out pretty quick. I guess it's the way we raised them—a participation trophy for everything. In our world, only first place gets a trophy."

Harner has found success in helping his Millennials see that they are part of a team, and that's a good thing, something many younger workers spark to. "Our team is a family," he told us. "So, if they work hard to get a car back on the track it could mean one more point, and that could lead to a championship for the team. They learn that the team is going to be behind them, and that's really positive. In turn, they have to work their butts off, so they don't let their team down."

In short, Harner has found that while managing younger workers may offer its unique challenges, he's not about to give up because the better he becomes at leading Millennials now the more returns his team will reap as they come to dominate the workforce.

The second big reason to devote special attention to younger workers is that, overgeneralizations aside, Millennials really *are* distinctive in some important ways that managers need to understand, which our research clearly reveals (Hint: It's more than beards on the men and yoga pants on the women). Understanding this handful of key distinguishing features about how Millennials prefer to work and what they are expecting from their managers and work lives is vital to assuring they work in harmony with their teammates. This understanding can also lead to best practices for inspiring Millennial workers' engagement and productivity, and even to convincing them to stay with the firm longer. That's essential, considering the troubling finding that less than one-third of Millennials feel their organization makes the most of their skills, and 66 percent expect to leave their employer in the next few years.

That threat of attrition is not an idle one. Millennials do leave jobs much faster than prior generations. We've come to calling this the *renter generation*. Millennials tend to rent their living quarters versus assuming a mortgage (desire for homeownership is on a sharp decline); they lease cars versus buying. They even rent boyfriends and girlfriends. Not in *that* way, but a steadily increasing number of twenty-somethings are shying away from traditional marriage and instead engaging in multiple short-term relationships. When they do get married, if they do, it's much later—now thirty on average for men and twenty-seven for women, compared with average ages of twenty-six and twenty-three just fifteen years ago. Pew Research estimates one-quarter of Millennials will never get married; almost half, in a recent *Time* magazine survey, said they would support a new marriage model that involved a two-year trial—a beta test if you will—at which point the union could be formalized or dissolved by either side with no divorce or paperwork required.

It's important to understand that a good deal of research on Millennials has shown that they are distrustful of institutions, marriage being just one of them. Opting out of the traditional marriage model in greater numbers could very well be attributable to the record high divorce rate of their parents. Many of them experienced the effects of such separations on their families, and virtually all witnessed those effects on the lives of friends.

That distrust of institutions is extending to the workplace. Many Millennials watched their parents go through rounds of downsizing, restructuring, reengineering, and M&A, that virtually eliminated the concept of job security. As such, many younger workers entering our teams today consider themselves to be renting their jobs; they aren't looking to buy. If things don't work out, they are indeed quite content to move on.

Melissa Aquino, vice president of the science and technology giant Danaher, calls Millennials one of the biggest diversity issues her 62,000 person company faces. While she personally believes this latest generation rocks, and has the potential to be the most productive in history, she acknowledges that organizations face a challenge in getting some of them to commit. "Millennials are largely critical of corporate America. They don't know if they want to be attached," she told us. More from Aquino in a moment.

Another reason for the fleet-footedness of Millennials: They were raised in an era of immediate gratification. Consider that this is the first generation to have grown up with such things as overnight delivery—no waiting a week for the postman to bring a package—and DVRs—they skip right through pesky TV commercials. Most never had to do research for school without the Internet— no need to trudge to the library and ponderously look up information. Of course, the ultimate provider of instant gratification is the smart phone. Who doesn't love their phone? Some 83 percent of Millennials report sleeping with their devices within reach so they don't miss out on messages during the night. But many Millennials use phones in distinctive ways from previous generations. For instance, they make much fewer voice calls. We have been told by younger employees that they believe phone calls to be rude— as if they are demanding a person's time at that precise moment. Moreover, they add, they often feel trapped on a call, giving their full attention to a glacially slow form of synchronous conversation.

As one Millennial told us in an interview, "If I could disable the phone on my phone, I would." (Paradoxically, we spoke with him while he worked at a retail phone store.)

Skanska USA CEO Rich Cavallaro explained that one way his company has appealed to people raised in a world of instant gratification is to ensure they have greater flexibility. "There's no question you have to manage this generation differently," he said. "We found forty-six percent of incoming employees from college say a flexible workplace is *the* most important thing for them." Yet, he admits, that's a challenge in a project-based business with 11,000 employees, but the company is striving hard to make it happen. "I come from a generation that if you weren't sitting at your desk, you weren't working: twelve hours a day, six days a week. That world is over. If we believe that we can tell Millennials to go sit at their desk all day, every day, we'll be here by ourselves."

As such, the company has launched the Skanska USA Flexible Work Program: finding ways to offer job sharing, flexible work time, telecommuting, a compressed work week, and part-time employment. And remember, this is a construction and development company, one that helped build the Oculus train station in New York City and is renovating LaGuardia Airport.

Leaders like Cavallaro teach us that we can't stick our fingers in our ears about generational disagreements anymore. This is reinforced by a study by the Society for Human Resource Management (SHRM), which found that nearly three quarters of HR professionals have reported not just differences but intergenerational *conflicts* in their organizations. We hear about them all the time in our consulting work: Managers and older workers complain about their younger colleagues' seemingly odd habits;

including a lack of commitment; and what they perceive as whiny demands for coaching, feedback, and praise. Millennials, in turn, have plenty of complaints about their bosses and older colleagues. The HR professionals surveyed by SHRM described the following most common negative perceptions:

MILLENNIALS TOP 3 COMPLAINTS ABOUT OLDER WORKERS

- Resistant to change
- Lack of recognition of my efforts
- Micromanage me

OLDER WORKERS TOP 3 COMPLAINTS ABOUT MILLENNIALS

- Poor work ethic
- Informal behavior and language
- Inappropriate dress

Melissa Aquino gets a chuckle out of that last complaint, the one about attire, but says it's something she considered when running an operating company at Danaher. "Whether right or wrong, Millennials are skeptical of older folks who dress too fancy," she said. So, as a nod to help her younger associates feel more included, and to help older workers loosen up, she presented company hoodies to everyone. "I handed one to our sixty-four-year-old finance guy who was wearing his tie. 'This is delightful,' he said, 'what am I supposed to do with it?'"

Overall, the good news we have about managing Millennials is twofold. First, we have identified a couple of key differences in what motivates them most strongly at work versus older workers, and we provide methods here for taking account of those motivators with specific management tactics that can dramatically boost their engagement. We've also found that Millennials share a particular set of strong motivators with older workers. In fact, the set of the top three motivators is fairly consistent across age groups, while the set of the lowest motivators has some similarities as well. So, as much as the differences in Millennials' preferences and behaviors are real and must be addressed, there also is a great deal of common ground with which to manage teams in ways that will bond younger workers and their older colleagues better to their teams, and also bond them more strongly with the organization overall.

THE BIG DIFFERENCES

One recent scholarly review concluded that there has been "limited research to guide managers on how to better incorporate the Millennial generation into the workplace." We are happy to step in. Let us dig a little deeper for you into our 50,000 person database. Respondents are employees of all ages, and are from the United States, Canada, Mexico, throughout Europe, Central and South America, Asia, Australia, the Middle East, and Africa. The database allows us unprecedented insight into what most motivates people at work, and what doesn't. Our Motivators Assessment ranks the twenty-three motivators—shown by our research to be most widely motivating for employees—all the way from the strongest to weakest for each person. We developed the Motivators Assessment with Drs. Jean Greaves and Travis Bradberry, creators of the *Emotional Intelligence 2.0* bestselling book and its accompanying assessment. These psychologists and their team of behavioral scientists helped us create a scientifically valid way of assessing people's underlying drivers at work.

For those curious about the complete set of twenty-three, here they are. You might want to see if you can guess which of them are most important to Millennials versus older generations.

Autonomy	Money
Challenge	Ownership
Creativity	Pressure
Developing Others	Prestige
Empathy	Problem Solving
Excelling	Purpose
Excitement	Recognition
Family	Service
Friendship	Social Responsibility
Fun	Teamwork
Impact	Variety
Learning	

Now, what did we find were the biggest differences? That's where we go next.

WHO WANTS TO WORK ALONE?

While autonomy ranks near the top set of motivators for older generations in the workplace, it's near the bottom of motivators for most younger workers. In fact, when we combined all answers from respondents in the Millennial generation, we found that autonomy ranked twenty-first overall (out of twenty-three motivators) for participants in that age group. However, autonomy was the eighth most important overall concept for Boomers and twelfth most important concept for Gen X. That's one of the single biggest shifts in the database, and it certainly bucks the prevailing wisdom that all workers thrive with more independence in their work. That was a central contention in Dan Pink's bestselling book *Drive*, in which he listed autonomy as *the* most important factor in motivating employees. The low desire for autonomy on the part of the vast majority of Millennials shows that it's time to differentiate the degree of independence we give to, and expect from, our employees.

This discrepancy alone can be one of the major sources of friction between Millennials and their bosses and older colleagues—and a key reason that older workers can find younger workers' requests for more direction, coaching, and inclusion to be irritating, or at the least counterintuitive. It's not unheard-of for some in the older generations to say that younger workers are acting immaturely, expecting so much hand-holding. But managers must understand that, for Millennials, it can be extremely frustrating not to have sufficient mentoring or time working in close collaboration with others.

Some managers hear this and assume this lack of self-governance is a serious shortcoming in their younger team members—something they need to get over. The better way to view it is as a terrific opportunity for building stronger teams. Where we think of Boomers and Gen Xers as largely *cowboys*—an individualistic lot—Millennials are *collaborators*. Said one Millennial: "Maybe it's our desire to be well-liked and to have a high friend count, but Millennials are great team players. Through school projects and massive, collaborative online games, we grew so comfortable working with others that many of us say we are more productive working in teams than on our own. This has obvious benefits in the workplace. Where other generations may have seen in teamwork only the danger that their hard work will not be rewarded and poor work will be blamed on a scapegoat, Millennials thrive on being part of a team."

All this means there is a seismic shift occurring in the workforce in how a lot of people want to work, which bodes well for the transition to the evolving network-of-teams approach. Leaders must assume many of their people now value being part of a meaningful team more than working independently. And a major implication is that if the team around them isn't meeting their collaboration and connectivity needs, Millennials are going to meet those needs elsewhere.

In one of our workshops, a forty-something team manager told us he was surprised to find one of his Millennial employees was crowdsourcing work problems online with friends. Let's say an important client wasn't returning calls from the young man; well, the worker posed this as a question to his network and asked for advice. In many cases, his friends responded in real-time on his social media sites, and often with workable ideas. He wasn't asking his boss because it took way too long to get a meeting, and that would involve an awkward face-to-face. This example bears up in a report from the University of North Carolina's Kenan-Flagler Business School, where researchers found many of today's workers don't see their managers as experts in subject areas the way their predecessors did. Why ask the boss when almost all the information you need is available online? Instead, the UNC researchers found, young workers want their managers to serve more as mentors and guides through the corporate experience.

This was revealing for the boss we spoke with. He realized he was not as relevant to his young employee's experience as he should be, nor were the employee's colleagues. The manager wasn't objecting to the notion that someone should consult his community of support for advice, it actually struck him as quite enterprising. But the employee's reliance on an outside network rather than those around the office certainly wasn't building loyalty to the team or company.

WILL YOU TELL ME HOW I'M DOING? PLEASE!

The second major difference we uncovered in the data is that Millennial employees are much more often strongly motivated by receiving recognition for their good work. In fact, overall, the data indicates that Millennials as a group are almost *twice* as likely to be motivated by recognition as Gen X and *three-and-a-half times* more likely to be motivated by recognition than Boomers. This might account for a lot of the irritation older bosses and colleagues tell us they feel about incessant requests from younger workers for feedback and praise.

The fact is that most Millennials have grown up with more recognition than any generation in history. Parents, teachers, coaches, and other nurturing bodies—only within the last few decades—embraced the practice of offering up a stream of continuous reinforcement. While Boomer and Gen X managers might find Millennials' demands for recognition and feedback annoying, it's ironic that most older folks acknowledge that they would have loved more of it from their parents. Many also admit, sheepishly, that they offered it in abundance to their kids—helping create the recognition junkies who are now emerging in the workforce. Younger people have had their finger paintings posted proudly on the fridge; collected gold, silver, and bronze stars on spelling papers; were named first chair in high school band or starting shortstop in softball; scored well in a round of debate and took home a ribbon. Even when their soccer team lost they beamed with joy at their participant medals. They've been dubbed the Everyone Gets a Trophy Generation. Technology has played a role too. Video games provide as many as 100 positive reinforcements a minute, while social media feeds provide a steady stream of reinforcing responses to pictures and comments. If a young woman wants to know if her friends think a new outfit is working for her, she can post a selfie straight from the dressing room and her tribe can gush. No wonder Millennials show up at work expecting at least a modicum of appreciation for their work. A boss telling them, "You don't get it yet, but you will. I'll let you know if you mess up, otherwise keep doing what you do!" feels like withdrawal.

So, with this new data on recognition and generations, we have begun pointing out to our clients the irony that they are spending the bulk of their time and money celebrating the accomplishments of more senior employees—those who hit big career milestones or do something above and beyond. It's not that those celebrations aren't worthwhile, nor should leaders stop them, but we must find ways to provide more meaningful, frequent recognition to our younger workers if we want to engage them and keep them.

While these differences in the expectations of Millennials about work have been a source of confusion or frustration to many managers and older colleagues, the fact is that on both counts they can push organizations in positive directions. As to recognition, while Millennials typically value it more than older workers, our research reveals that appreciation of achievements is a powerful driver of engagement and commitment for just about everybody.

Dan Helfrich came to see the power of frequent, sincere recognition as an attribute of a healthy team culture. The leader of Deloitte's 8,500 person Federal Government Services Practice told us he conducted an experiment. "I knew our people were doing great things for each other every day, so I sent an email asking them to reply with the story of someone who had helped them, and to copy the person. In one week, we had a thousand recognition emails. I realized, 'Holy cow, our culture is so supportive of one another.' But I also realized we had tapped into a nerve of people who wanted to say thank you more and weren't."

Helfrich said he was awed by, "the swelling of pride that our people felt from a three-line email that was copied to the overall leader of the business saying, 'Robin did something amazing last week.' It was this spontaneous thing that started an amazing conversation in our team about the power of gratitude."

The point for us: Recognition not only helps retain and engage Millennials, but is energizing for employees of all ages.

The same is true about fostering more collaborative and inclusive problem solving, as opposed to emphasizing autonomy. While the greatest admiration in our workplaces has typically gone to the lone hero who solves the problem, wins the big deal, and calms the angry customer, the payoffs of collaboration are so numerous that fostering shared responsibility and developing better ways of working closely together is essential.

Thus, team leaders have a marvelous opportunity, as they seek to manage Millennials better, to shift perspectives about how all team members should work overall.

What we found next, is that Millennials are also pushing teams in positive directions when it comes to the major motivators that they *share* with their elders.

CAPITALIZING ON THE COMMONALITIES

As our research team sorted through our database, one of the most striking findings was how similar people are in the top and bottom motivators across all four generations. While there was quite a lot of variation in motivators four to twenty between age groups, the top three were exactly the same for all groups until we reach the Traditionalists (those born before 1945). The bottom three were also remarkably similar, but had a few important exceptions.

Take a look at this snapshot of the top and bottom three for each generation:

TOP 3 MOTIVATORS

Millennials:	1. Impact	2. Learning	3. Family
Gen X:	1. Impact	2. Learning	3. Family
Boomers:	1. Impact	2. Learning	3. Family
Traditionalists:	1. Impact	2. Learning	3. Creativity

BOTTOM 3 MOTIVATORS

Millennials:	21. Prestige	22. Autonomy	23. Money
Gen X:	21. Fun	22. Prestige	23. Money
Boomers:	21. Fun	22. Prestige	23. Money
Traditionalists:	21. Recognition	22. Prestige	23. Money

It's in order to provide a little explanation of how our research team defined some of these motivators. The desire for *impact* is the need to know that your work is important and makes a positive difference in the world. Just to underscore the significance of this idea, it is the number one ranked motivator for every age group from the Gen Z teens who've taken the assessment to working adults over the age of seventy.

As for the desire for *learning*, it might appear fairly straight-forward—it's the wish to keep developing our talents and increasing our knowledge. This idea has appeared in other surveys by other researchers, but we've looked under the hood to find that similar labels can mask important differences based on age. The most effective learning for Millennials is often collaborative and tech-forward. For Boomers, the best learning typically builds on their experience and knowledge (versus being completely new to them). It also should be immediately applicable to their work. For older employees, learning also comes through variety, and variety as a motivator grows substantially in importance with age. Variety moves from a middle of the pack concept for Millennials (ranked eleventh) to one of the strongest motivators for people later in their careers (fourth for Boomers). Thus, for older workers—who many leaders, unfortunately, take for granted—a sure way to disconnect them is to have their work become rote.

Next, with *family*, our research shows people who are motivated by this concept feel it's important to balance work and personal time, and they want to make their loved ones' proud of them. An interesting note: This motivator was number one for Millennial women.

Overall, more Millennials stand out as being especially closely bonded to their parents in comparison with prior generations. It's not too far from reality to say that the majority of Boomers and Gen Xers would have lived in a cardboard box before moving back in with mom and dad after college, but now it's commonplace. Many Millennials allow their parents into their social media worlds, text them, and communicate in some way with them almost daily. Again, to show how a similar label might mask generational differences: For older workers, family often means kids and/ or spouse or partner. More important than daily work/life balance for many in older generations is leaving a legacy of what they value to their children.

You won't see many other research studies showing mom and dad or husband or wife as a driver of productivity or motivation. It might be a little uncomfortable to consider family as a motivator in our buttoned-down business teams, but it's not a bad thing. Not at all. There's a large body of research that suggests employees working long hours—subsequently ignoring those important to them outside the job, like family—does not help companies. It doesn't seem to result in more output. In a fascinating study by Erin Reid, a professor at Boston University's Questrom School of Business, managers could not tell the difference at all in output between employees who worked eighty hours a week and those who just pretended to. And Reid was not able to find any evidence that those employees who worked a normal week accomplished less, or any sign that the overworking employees accomplished more.

Moreover, considerable evidence shows that overwork is not just neutral, it can hurt workers and their companies. Marianna Virtanen of the Finnish Institute of Occupational Health found that overwork and resulting stress can lead to health problems including impaired sleep, depression, heavy drinking, diabetes, impaired memory, and heart disease. None of those are good for an employee or a company's bottom line. They show up in increased absenteeism, attrition, and health insurance costs. Even the stingiest of bosses, who cares nothing for his employees' personal well-being, should find some compelling signs that there are real, balance-sheet costs incurred when employees ignore their personal lives.

Overall, we see that while there are important insights that come out of this data, that many Millennials tend to be especially vocal about their desire to make an impact and to learn and to have time for family, they are in fact voicing the deepest desires of people of all ages (just perhaps more vocally). The majority of workers want these things. Thus, leaders who incorporate methods of satisfying Millennials' demands are going to be better managers of everyone else too.

If we apply what we learn with this data, we find Millennials will help push teams in positive directions. Providing more explicitly designed opportunities to take on challenges to grow and develop, helping people see the larger value of the work they're doing—and balancing time with their loved ones—may be especially important for Millennials. But doing so will also reap great rewards in increased engagement for the rest of the team as well.

Thus, we present here a handful of key strategies we found that not only motivate Millennial workers more strongly, but which our research shows can energize people of all ages. The strategies are:

- Adopt simple rituals of recognition
- Institute transparency about collective team challenges

- Foster directly relevant learning
- Clearly articulate to the team the meaning of their work

We'll take a close look at each in turn.

ADOPT SIMPLE RITUALS OF RECOGNITION

Not long ago we were conducting a training at a Silicon Valley technology company. When we explained that research shows the most engaged Millennials are recognized more often, and that this particular company's employee engagement survey showed its recognition scores were, *ahem*, kind of sucky, one man countered with: "My first boss didn't say good job very often, but when he did you knew he meant it." We asked the rest of the group for their thoughts, and a woman spoke up: "That may have worked for you, Rod, but act like that today and your programmers will leave you." Many of those in the room nodded their heads in agreement. We could tell by his expression that Rod wasn't sold, and you might not be either. Many managers tell us that recognition is not motivating to them (and so assume it's not for their people), some are too busy to find the time, others are worried about jealousies arising if one person is recognized and others aren't, some say they don't know what to give for what achievements, the explanations go on and on. Let us share with you some powerful data on the value of this idea. Deloitte has found productivity, performance, and employee engagement are, on average, 14 percent higher in teams where employees feel regularly recognized for their work. Our 200,000 person research study for our book *The Carrot Principle* showed organizations that are most effective at recognizing excellence were three times more profitable (as measured by operating profit margin) than those that gave little to no recognition.

That said, let us make one thing clear: No manager will ever be perfect at appreciating their employees' work. You'll never catch everyone, say the right thing every time, give the perfect awards. But the alternative—skipping it entirely—is the managerial equivalent of punting on first down (squandering an ample opportunity).

Recognition, after all, is about more than expressing gratitude. It is perhaps the most powerful teaching tool a manager has at her disposal. One of a manager's most pressing jobs is to stay on top of problems. What we find is that managers can prevent a lot of issues from ballooning into problems by publicly calling attention to those small things her people are doing well—pointing everyone in the right direction in a positive way—and especially those bigger things people are doing that are exceptional, that are above and beyond. Each recognition moment with an employee or team is a chance to communicate vital information—to those receiving the award and those around them. This is especially important in helping Millennials know they are making an impact.

Offering regular recognition doesn't have to take a lot of time. The most effective managers in our studies spend only about an hour a week, on average, recognizing the accomplishments of their people—that's about two percent of a fifty-hour work week. Yet they have significantly higher employee engagement scores and much lower attrition. Even brief expressions of appreciation, when done frequently, can lead to extraordinary gains in worker satisfaction and commitment.

So, below, we offer our Top Seven Ways to provide recognition, culled from decades consulting with organizations about their recognition strategies:

7 WAYS TO OFFER SMART RECOGNITION

1. **APPLAUD ATTEMPTS:** Good bowlers don't aim for the pins but for the arrows set on the lane fifteen feet from the foul line. This is called *spot bowling*. A ball that rolls over the right spot (or arrow) will usually continue down a straight path and hit the right pin. In great teams, managers aim their people at regular, small-scale milestones to get to the big ones, and they praise every positive step taken along the way—including valiant efforts that don't work out (workplace gutter balls, if you will). For the 2013–17 seasons, the Philadelphia 76ers basketball team had one of the worst records in the National Basketball Association, yet the sales team set league records for season-ticket sales. They created an environment where teammates were constantly praised and applauded for what they call *hustle stats*—not dollars booked but all the little things that lead to a sale. That included time on the phone, emails sent, face time with clients in person, online connections made, coaching other teammates, and so on. Employees with the most hustle points earned public praise in huddles, had their names flashed on flat screens around the office, and could earn wacky, fun team prizes—like rotating championship wrestling belts, golden boots, and bronze wolf statues—for their efforts.

2. **DO IT NOW:** Kind of like milk left out of the fridge, thank-you does not keep long. The closer recognition is given to the

time a behavior happens, the more a manager reinforces the behavior and employees learn what matters most in the team. Many leaders think they'll remember employee achievements, perhaps believing them more appropriate to reinforce in the next performance review, but too often the acts are forgotten and the chance to reinforce is lost— along with the motivating power for other team members to witness the celebratory events. Timeliness is especially important with Millennials, satisfying their desire for instant gratification. Lance Trenary, CEO of Golden Corral, is a big believer in the timeliness of recognition. To that end, he has provided the system with golden nuggets to hand out as soon as they see coworkers doing something great. Managers can add a few lines of gratitude on to these nugget-shaped thank-you notes, or also include a gold-nugget lapel pin. Trenary adds, however, that even with tools to facilitate speed-to-recognition, a manager, "Has to find out what's important to the individual. Some people like verbal praise, others a gold nugget, someone else wants half a day off in summer to spend with their kids."

3. **DO IT OFTEN:** We've found members of the most engaged teams report feeling some form of appreciation from their leader or fellow teammates about once a week. Yet a lot of leaders worry they could end up giving out *too much* recognition. Really? Have you ever worked at a place that appreciated you too much? Royal Bank of Canada (RBC) has an award-winning online system where employees and managers can post electronic recognition that can be viewed by the entire 80,000 person workforce. Little and big wins are broadcast

for everyone to see and be inspired by the stories—and they have been happening multiple times a day around the banking system for several years now. RBC also encourages co-workers to add an electronic thumbs-up or a short comment of encouragement. This constant, frequent flow of social appreciation is helping build a culture of frequent gratitude throughout the bank, and reinforces the concept that every role is important if we are going to win as a team.

4. **BE SPECIFIC:** Generic praise has little to no meaning for employees. We've probably all known a boss who sprayed the place with meaningless platitudes like, "Good job, everyone." He thought he was being magnanimous, but came off a bit clueless, as though he had no idea what his people were really doing. The hard truth is some team members might not have done that good a job, while others have made truly stellar contributions. The result of this style of leveling-praise can lead to cynicism. A team leader of an engineering design team told us he learned this the hard way. Jennifer, he said, was, "by far my most innovative and productive designer. And she got along with everyone, and that's not always the case with high performers in our business." The problem was, the manager didn't want to praise Jennifer too much in front of the team because she was *always* the best. "Frankly, Jeff worked right next to Jennifer, and I didn't want him to feel bad." The manager summed it up, "Over time I think Jennifer felt undervalued. She left for a competitor a while ago." When we asked if Jeff was still there, the manager nodded. Of course. Jeff wasn't going anywhere. A lesson learned.

5. **CLEARLY REINFORCE KEY VALUES**: The most effective teams typically operate under a brief list of core values or guiding principles, and their leaders are constantly on the lookout for members who demonstrate them. With public recognition, they reinforce those behaviors to the entire team. We get a chance to work with a lot of great organizations, and the best always have clear values. Johnson & Johnson's credo is etched into limestone in the HQ lobby—putting customers at the top, employees second, and shareholders last. But anyone who's owned J&J shares long enough knows that a fantastic return has come from living these values in this order. At Tesco, Europe's largest retailer, the core values can be easily found in every store, lorry, and online location. Team members have little trouble reciting the three: "No one tries harder for customers," "We treat people how they want to be treated," and "Every little help makes a big difference." These concepts are brought up in team meetings before shifts; and when managers recognize associates, the celebrations are focused on one of the three specific behaviors.

6. **FORMALLY CELEBRATE SIGNIFICANT OUTCOMES**: When a big goal is reached, it can be demotivating for a manager to offer up only *attaboys,* such as: "You saved our biggest account, Nadine. Here's a Starbucks card. Let me know if you get change." Great managers know they have to *celebrate* outcomes with an award and a presentation that is meaningful to the person. The award may be something intangible—from the assignment of a leadership role on a big project, to time off to be with friends or family—to something tangible like a formal award. It depends, again, on the person and what they

value. At Rich Product Corporation in Buffalo, the brand promise is to treat customers, associates, and communities like family. As such, the company has celebrated the success of its best individual performers and teams with a vacation in the Rich family jet. (That's the kind of family we want to be a part of.) The trips created ambassadors within the associate ranks who spread the word that good works are recognized. Of course, most of us can't give out rides in our private Gulfstreams, but it's not a stretch to find an award that will be meaningful to an individual and somewhat commensurate with an accomplishment.

7. **TAKE A STEP**: In formally presenting an award, managers can add impact by remembering the acronym STEP: Tell a **S**tory about the accomplishment, gather the immediate team **T**ogether to listen and add comments (recognition is always public, criticism is private), **E**mphasize a core value that has been demonstrated, and **P**ersonalize the moment. Public recognition like this happens regularly at Tire Kingdom Service Centers. In just one circumstance, a district manager told us he'd recognized one of his general service technicians. The manager said: "He executed the inspection process correctly and turned in the inspection within the time rule, which is the key to this process. I brought the entire team into a quick huddle, thanked the team for their hard work and for keeping the brand-new store clean every day. I reviewed what the associate did and why it was important and then presented him with a thank-you card and a twenty-five-dollar gift card." And yet the touching moment for the district manager came about thirty minutes

later when the associate came and asked him to sign and date the card on the front because he wanted to put it in a frame. Why was this simple act so powerful? Because the associate's peers were gathered and a manager explained exactly why he was being recognized. Great business leaders create similar moments for their people by taking just a few minutes to think about how to best deliver each award.

INSTITUTE TRANSPARENCY ABOUT COLLECTIVE TEAM CHALLENGES

Being more transparent with your team about problems as they arise, how the team can step up, who's tasked with doing what, and the perception of higher-ups about team performance are among the most powerful ways to help younger workers feel they are valuable contributors and part of a collective effort. With such transparency, not only Millennials, but everyone, can see better how the team fits into the larger operation, not to mention understand how they might make more impactful contributions. Being more transparent empowers all members of a team.

Joe Badaracco, professor of business ethics at Harvard Business School, advises managers, "If you find yourself being furtive too often—editing a lot of what you say before you say it, or being secretive with information, hiding things from people—I'd stop and ask what is really going on. It may be time to take a step back and do some reflection." If your people don't know what's going wrong, how can they possibly help you fix it?

Transparency is particularly important to Millennials. Danaher

Vice President Aquino told us she's tried to implement solutions for this in her team. She said, "Boomers want to be honored for their legacy and what they know, Millennials want information. They are used to living in a world of perfect information and, if it's not, they often don't get started. I'd estimate this generation can give twenty percent more productivity than any generation if they have the right information to get started."

So, she tells her new hires to not be intimidated but to seek out knowledge. "I give each of my new people a list of five people they need to meet and the core knowledge those people have. They are supposed to set up meetings, meet with them face-to-face, and interview them. Then they come back and give me a summary of what they learned. That's led to some really rich discussions."

Aquino is among the team leaders we've met who are transforming their workplaces from need-to-know cultures to need-to-share, where privacy is being replaced with a permanent transparency. In our personal lives, most likely because of social media, more of us are living in the open than ever before, and this is transferring rapidly into the work world. Secrecy, once considered the accepted norm in business, is now largely anachronistic. Who would have ever believed that employees would get to rate their bosses in public, which they can on Glassdoor and other sites—or their customers—encouraged in places like Airbnb and Uber. Who could have predicted a new Pope's first charge to his Vatican administrators would be "absolute transparency" (as we saw with Pope Francis).

Millennials have grown up with the belief they have an inalienable right to participate, and smart managers are encouraging it, and it's leading their teams to be more collaborative as a result. Participating in decision-making tends to reduce stress, increase trust, and create a culture where people are more likely to own challenges and solutions. We instinctively know how important this kind of transparency is in our personal lives. We wouldn't fall in love with someone if they failed to disclose as we got to know them better. As hunky as James Bond might be, most women would not put up with his clandestine behavior for long. Similarly, in our work lives, we don't create a connection with a manager who keeps everything close to the vest.

There's a propensity to think of this idea of transparency as something to do when a mistake has been made. While that is an important part of the process—fessing up when we mess up—we are speaking of *proactive* transparency. For example, consider why so many hip restaurants nowadays allow customers to see their chefs at work, and the cooks to see their customers. Is this simply for better ambiance? Hardly. A study by Harvard Business School researchers found a 17 percent increase in customer satisfaction with food and 13 percent faster service in these open environments. In this literally transparent world of dining, customers feel as if they are part of the creative process, and workers seem to be more thoughtful and precise knowing that they are observed.

Transparency about who is doing what tasks, and how it's all going, is fundamental if team members are going to assist one another. That can create better connections with younger workers and their older colleagues. After all, longer tenured workers do tend to have more connections within the organization and ways of getting information, and younger workers can often offer disruptive ideas and solutions, especially those using technology.

A few questions a manager might ask herself about the amount of transparency she's fostering are:

- Do I share everything about our team with my employees, or do I find myself keeping information secret that doesn't need to be?
- Do we have a very clear way to post our team goals and current performance levels for all to see?
- Am I consistent about involving my people in decision-making with issues that affect their work lives?
- Do my employees have a say in setting goals that are important in their jobs?
- What avenues do my team members have to voice their ideas and concerns?
- How do I show my employees their opinions and ideas are appreciated?

Kim Cochran is regional sales manager for Fluke Industrial Group, a manufacturer of electronic test tools and software. She took over her nine-state region three years ago, at a time when the company was losing too many of its valuable technical salespeople. One of her first steps as manager was to review the latest engagement survey results for her new team, and found that half her people were actively looking for another job.

Jump ahead three years, and Cochran hasn't lost a single one.

She credits the biggest change in her team with implementing an extraordinary degree of transparency. Her people are all remote, and they travel nonstop. Thus, her goal is to help them feel included and listened to, but never overwhelmed by information. She therefore classifies all messages that come in to her on a ladder.

On the lowest rung are things that she can take care of for

her direct reports without bothering them. These are easy. Boom, done.

The next rung up involves information that does need her employees' attention, but isn't going to make or break their sales efforts—things such as due dates for benefits sign-up or when sales forecasts are due. She sends these out in a short email. Her people know she tries to screen the information that comes their way; thus an email from Cochran does need some attention. "The trick is not to harp on them," she says. "That can be frustrating for people who are busy. Things do accidentally fall off their radar." The goal is to keep her people on schedule and watch out for them.

Next up the ladder comes information she classifies as hot topics, those items that her folks will need to give serious attention—changes in work process, organizational structure, pay plan, customer pricing, and so on. During the week she compiles these issues on a running agenda and brings them up one by one in her weekly open-forum call with the entire team. These weekly calls can get heated, and she says, "There are times I have to say, 'There's more to come on this topic, but I'm not at liberty to share right now,' or, 'I know this is a problem, and I want to assure you that it is being looked at from a very high level.'"

Cochran says she's tried to do a better job of communicating the *why* behind decisions made above them. "If we roll out a new sales process, for instance, as a manager I'll be privy to all the whys and hows. But I'm rolling it out to fresh ears on my team. I have to explain, 'This is *why* we are doing this, here are the statistics that show why it's important,' versus 'This is what we are going to do.'" If there's debate, she promises her team that she'll raise the issues with her higher-ups and find resolutions, if possible.

The top step in her ladder approach is information classified as urgent—those 911 items that can't wait even a day to share. In this case, Cochran will call a huddle phone call at day's end (when most associates are available). "I've learned this should not be used for everyday topics, since it puts everyone in the fire-drill mode constantly. I have been a part of an organization like that, and it's miserable," she said.

One of our favorite stories of transparency comes from Quicken Loans, where a handful of the 10,000 employees accidentally call CEO Bill Emerson every month. He doesn't mind. He has given his personal cell-phone number to each employee, and expects a few pocket dials now and then.

"It's an open culture," he says. "I encourage leaders to be accessible because it breeds an inclusive culture." And as the senior-most leader, Emerson realizes he must model the behavior. The CEO only receives a handful of real calls from employees each month (even some from brave interns), and most are about regular business. He has not yet received any prank calls. Still, he does remember a few unusual moments.

During one new employee orientation session, new hires were given an awareness quiz, which came soon after Emerson and founder Dan Gilbert spent a ten-hour day going over Quicken's ISMs (values) and culture. In the quiz, one of the questions was, 'What color are Bill Emerson's eyes?' "I got like six phone calls from people asking if I would answer the question for them. I'm like, 'Are you kidding me? I can't answer that; it's an *awareness* quiz!'"

So, we find with a smile, there may be a few times when it's not good to be too transparent—even in the most transparent of cultures.

MILLENNIAL STRATEGY C

FOSTER DIRECTLY RELEVANT LEARNING AND CAREER DEVELOPMENT

We introduced you to Skanska USA earlier in this chapter. Leaders at this firm have found they must create regular learning experiences for Millennials, so they have started rotating new, young hires every six months until they find their sweet spot in this construction giant. In the rotations, employees will usually have roles in safety, estimating, quality, and as superintendents on various projects.

The company has also changed the way their people learn—again due to the Millennial influence. Says CEO Rich Cavallaro, "If the taillight goes out on my wife's 2012 Jeep Cherokee, how do I fix it? I watch a video on YouTube and in ten minutes I can do the job. If I didn't have that video, it would take me three hours to figure out how to remove all the parts. That's how people learn now." And, as such, Skanska's process to bring people up to speed has become much more video based, offered in bite-sized increments.

Mitch Snyder, CEO of 7,000 person Bell Helicopter, finds his Millennials need much more feedback about career development. "When I started years ago, we got a promotion every two years—from an associate to an engineer to a lead engineer to a senior engineer. Then someone decided no, you are an engineer and that's it. But Millennials value nurturing and constant high-level engagement with their leaders, as well as being challenged and making a difference. They need to feel there is a path for their career." Thus, Bell has become more transparent about career development and lateral and promotional opportunities, and encourages mentoring sessions with managers to help employees take each step forward.

That kind of frequent interaction with leaders is at the heart of how most people learn. In fact, a commonly used formula within the training profession is what's called the 70:20:10 model. It's used to describe the optimal sources of learning for workers, and holds that individuals obtain roughly 70 percent of their work knowledge from job-related experiences, 20 percent from interactions with influential others (like mentors and coaches), and 10 percent from formal educational events.

The 70:20:10 model's developers—Morgan McCall, Michael Lombardo, and Robert Eichinger—were researchers at the Center for Creative Leadership. They held that hands-on experience (the 70 percent) is the most beneficial for employees because it enables them to discover and refine their job-related skills on the fly, understand customers better, make decisions and address challenges, see how products are made, and interact in real-time with bosses and coworkers within actual work settings. Individuals can also learn from their mistakes and receive immediate feedback on performance.

Employees learn from others (the 20 percent) through a variety of activities that include social learning, coaching, mentoring, collaborative learning, and other methods of interaction with peers. Encouragement and feedback are prime benefits of this valuable learning approach.

To help accomplish this type of learning, we watched with interest recently as ten senior leaders from Michigan Medicine (formerly the University of Michigan Health System) started something called MicroMentors in their organization. The idea was to provide emerging leaders at this 26,000 person healthcare organization a way to spend up to sixty minutes of undivided attention with a senior leader. These short, one-time bursts of mentoring assist emerging leaders in working through issues with someone who has experience in the area. There's no long-term relationship expected. Topics offered include everything from managing disruptive employee behavior to better determining your team's priorities, from strategic planning to salary negotiation, from building high-functioning teams to managing stress and balancing work and home. The most oft-requested micromentoring sessions have revolved around career development—with younger leaders asking questions of their micromentors about pursuing additional education or trying new things in their careers. And since the executives involved want to retain these high-potential employees, they can usually point out opportunities available by staying and growing within Michigan Medicine. It's a terrific idea.

Finally, the 70:20:10 formula holds that only about one-tenth of professional development comes from traditional instruction and educational events, a finding that typically surprises those with academic backgrounds (but literally no one else). Now, with that said, formal training is still foundational in providing a vital overview of concepts from proven sources, presented in creative ways that employees and managers can begin to process. Companies invest a lot in corporate universities, learning programs, and leadership development training, and there's no doubt the teams and leaders we work with are hungry for these kinds of opportunities. But, we've found, team leaders must also be active in fostering learning. You can't just ship employees off to a class and hope they grow into the dream contributors you need.

The Philadelphia 76ers sales team, with 105 people, is the largest in the National Basketball Association—and Millennials comprise 99 percent of the group. "They want to run through walls, they want to change the world," said CEO Scott O'Neil. The sales team uses a two-week onboarding process to immerse young new professionals in the office's sales process, but learning doesn't stop there.

"In other places, I trained for a few weeks and then it was survival of the fittest," said Evan Ostrosky, manager of inside sales. "Here, we train our reps at least once or twice a week on everything and anything. For example, if a player gets injured, we'll get everyone together and train so we all have the same exact message." Weekly, managers will also take a group of reps through mock appointments, techniques in finding their voice and understanding customer needs, and how to tell better stories. "Many millennials leave because they don't feel challenged after a year," said Ostrosky. "We want to develop you the entire time you are here. And not just about sales, we want to grow you professionally and as a person."

Another company that's good at creating relevant and engaging opportunities to learn throughout an employee's tenure is DreamWorks Pictures—creators of animated hits like *Shrek*, *How to Train Your Dragon*, and *Kung Fu Panda*. DreamWork's thirteen-acre campus more resembles a small liberal arts college than a business, and many employees resemble college students. Nearly a quarter of the 2,200 workers are under thirty, and the studio has a 97 percent retention rate. The strategy here: Foster spontaneous discussions, encourage risk-taking, openly discuss mistakes, share successes, and nurture professional development.

As part of that, all new hires are encouraged to develop and pitch a movie idea to members of the executive team. The company even offers workshops and mentoring on how to make the pitches successful. DreamWorks has also invested in a robust education department, offering various classes to help employees develop not only their business acumen but artistic skills, such as photography, sculpting, painting, improv, and cinematography, which they can take during work hours.

While this is a terrific example of effective formal education, we again stress how important direct manager involvement is in the career development process. The format we advise for this is holding regular aspirational conversations, which we'll discuss in the next chapter, short career discussions with those employees who work for you. Generally, having one of these conversations once a month with direct reports and at least once or twice a year with skip-level employees is optimal. But in some high turnover industries, such as retail or service, a best-practice shows holding them weekly can cut turnover as much as in half.

MILLENNIAL STRATEGY D

CLEARLY ARTICULATE TO THE TEAM THE MEANING OF THEIR WORK

Philosopher Frederick Nietzsche is quoted as saying, "He who has a *why* to live for can endure almost any *how*." And, we'd add, he can endure much better the setbacks that inevitably happen (the *what the hecks!*). Theodore Seuss Geisel (Dr. Seuss) was rejected by twenty-seven publishers before he sold his first book—and then 600 million copies more. Unable to have children of his own,

Seuss found a great sense of meaning by helping other people raise their kids with tolerance and love for humanity. Oprah Winfrey thought she wanted to be a newscaster and became the co-anchor of a nightly network affiliate in Baltimore when just twenty-two. She was fired from that job, probably because—as she recalls—her heart wasn't in it. She wanted to inspire people to be more than they thought they ever could be. Once she launched her talk show, she was fulfilling her personal mission.

The power of *why* was on thrilling display at the Euro 2016 Football (soccer) Championship in France. The best men's national teams from across Europe battled for the title of the continent's best and, after the group stage, powerhouse England was set to play upstart Iceland in the knockout round. To put this match into perspective, Iceland is a country of 330,000 people; it has more volcanoes than professional soccer players, and one of the head coaches is a practicing dentist. The entire English national team play for clubs that are household names such as Manchester United, Arsenal, and Liverpool. Meanwhile, Iceland's players suit up in places like Israel and Turkey for clubs like the Grasshoppers and Whalers. Odds-makers predicted the Brits would win by at least four goals.

But Iceland was playing to bring pride and joy to the tiny country. More than 10 percent of the entire population journeyed to France for the tournament, and 98 percent of the rest tuned in on television. And as they had progressed through the set of matches, after each game, the players and coaches put on an exhilarating display of appreciation for their fans. In unison on the sidelines, the team began a slow, overhead clap, leading their supporters in the stands. They called this Viking Thunder Clap, and it was punctuated with a guttural "huh" as the hands came together. Slowly the clapping built in momentum until thousands of Icelandic voices were roaring, hands clapping wildly, creating a cacophony of sound that floated out of the stadiums and filled the French streets. Unless your team had just lost to the Icelanders, it was impossible not to be moved by the display.

In their knockout game with England, Iceland stunned the football world by winning 2–1.

We acknowledge that the argument for a strong sense of meaning—clarity around an inspiring *why*—has been a staple of management books recently. You'd think by now that most managers would be following the advice. Apparently, it's not that easy. Try this experiment with your team. With no prompting about the right answer, ask each employee individually to write down what they believe the core purpose of your team is, answering the questions: Why does our specific team exist / why do we get up and come into work every day? If all the answers are pretty much the same, and exactly what you'd want them to say, your team passes with flying colors and you can skip the rest of this chapter. But we've done this exercise with many, many teams—even those you would think have a clear purpose such as a nonprofit—and the answers usually range dramatically.

Failing to define a clear and compelling *why* is squandering a golden opportunity to create a strong bonding force among team members of all ages. We emphasize that this is one key way to unify younger workers and their older colleagues and bridge the gaps between. Believing in a noble cause makes older workers more willing to spend time mentoring younger team members and be more open to sharing with them. For Millennials (who we often call the Why Generation), clarity about the cause helps them believe that, even as entry-level players, they are making a significant contribution to a mission that matters.

Now, we understand there can still be skepticism about the value of crafting a team statement of purpose—*Ah, motherhood and apple pie*, some cynics claim. And the detractors are not too far from the truth in some cases. Many team statements tend to be too generic to do much good: "Customers come first." *Really, how?* Others are too mind-numbingly dull to have any inspirational effect: "We have committed to engineer excellent solutions while promoting personal employee growth." *Doesn't everyone?* While some are so complex as to baffle an astrophysicist: "We will disseminate error-free solutions and endeavor to monetize performance-based benefits while continuing to continually facilitate progressive meta-services." *So stirring. We might have to borrow a hanky (sniff).*

There are a few mission statement generators on the Web if you need a good laugh, and Weird Al Yankovic's parody song "Mission Statement" is well worth a listen.

Scott Weisberg, chief people officer for The Wendy's Company, admits he's been a bit of a cynic too: "I'm about to sound a bit like Scrooge, but I'm an HR guy who hasn't seen the value of taking a great deal of senior leadership time to develop a 'vision.' Too often it ends up getting shelved or it's not actionable. That said, I've always been a believer in people understanding the *purpose* of everything they do."

As such, Wendy's executive team met not long ago to reflect on its own purpose. To be clear, the senior leadership team wasn't trying to define the overall purpose of Wendy's, but the reason the executive team existed. What job could this group of senior leaders do that no one else could? What they came up with were two words: joy and opportunity. Said Weisberg, "We realized our job is to bring *joy* to people's lives through our customer experience and provide an *opportunity* for our team members to grow."

There can be brilliance in simplicity, when it's as good as that.

To avoid the generic, complex, or dull, there are a few keys to making the exercise of creating a team purpose statement most meaningful. The first step is to encourage input from your team, meaning, "Don't do this alone." With that said, we do not recommend asking your team the question: "What's our purpose?" Instead, make it more human by asking, "Why do we exist as a team?" or "What job do we do for customers?" or "What gets you excited to come here every day?"

In answering these questions, employees can be in the same room, but should draft their attempts independently. Working together on a first draft typically ends up with a synergized mess where the team, "Leverages its core competencies to *blah blah*." The process works best this way: Draft alone, then decide together. A good facilitator, from outside the group (maybe from HR, L&D, or communications—if you have those functions) can help cull the best ideas and then weave them into a compelling, yet brief, manifesto.

We were working with the IT department of a large bank, which had an overall corporate mission to make customers' financial lives more successful. Surveys showed team members in the IT team, however, weren't clear as to how their work impacted that big mission—since they never saw or spoke with live customers. They met as a team and came up with a purpose: "We *enable* great customer experiences." That might not seem too sexy, but the word "enable" meant a lot to this group of programmers, system architects, and help-desk staff. The IT folks then developed a list of "enablers"—specific behaviors they expected from each other. Those included such things as: "We anticipate and act with urgency," "We empower people to take action," and "We are courageous." Finally, under each enabler, they then came up with specific definitions and examples to help associates understand "What it looks like" and "What I can do today." So, for example, under the enabler "We are courageous," associates could read in the definitions and examples that it was okay and expected to ask tough questions of each other and their managers, strongly advocate for their customers, and challenge the status quo in processes and design.

That level of specificity helped these information technology workers better understand their unique roles, how they could make the bank great, and truly help customers' financial lives through their work behind the scenes writing code, fixing computers, and managing the network.

We've conducted this kind of purpose exercise with hundreds of teams. One of our favorite cases was working with Dr. John Charpie, director of the Michigan Medicine's Congenital Heart Center, and his team, which comprises a few dozen nurses, physicians, researchers, techs, and environmental services professionals who take care of very sick children with heart problems. The purpose statement Charpie led his team to was: "Our job is to turn our patients' and their families' worst day into their best day." Now that's a source of unity and inspiration.

Another great example we found was at TCC Wireless, the

nation's largest Verizon reseller. The company has hundreds of stores nationwide with 2,900 employees—85 percent of whom are Millennials. But TCC's turnover is 20 percent below the national average for retailers, employee engagement is at record highs, as are profits.

Ryan McCarty was a pastor when TCC hired him to create a social responsibility initiative that would help the young employees feel the company was giving back. They ended up calling it a *Culture of Good*. McCarty explained it this way, "We wanted to create a place where you go to work every day and can be a force for good; that by working together with their customers and communities, employees can truly change the world." Amen, Pastor!

They started with backpacks. The first fall, McCarty and the team at TCC filled 60,000 backpacks with much-needed school supplies, then they distributed the packs to employees in twenty-eight states. McCarty asked team members to get involved in finding kids in need and distributing them. Note that he didn't ask just the store managers to do this, but everyone.

Said the former pastor: "When word got out about the backpacks our employees were handing out, people in need began to show up. Kids were hugging employees, parents had tears of gratitude." How do you think TCC's workforce felt getting up the next day? No snooze button for them.

Today, Culture of Good has quarterly activities—and each store has the independence to do what their employees think will do the most good in their communities. Workers also receive sixteen hours a year paid time off to do good on their own. And, corporatewide, the Backpack Giveaway is now an annual tradition.

Now, they give away (with help from other corporate partners) about 300,000 backpacks.

The result of a heightened focus on meaning? About 70 percent of employees believe the Culture of Good has won them new customers. But, more important, there's an authenticity here that tells us everyone believes it's the right thing to do.

McCarty said, "We are not trying to turn our company into a nonprofit. We want to be successful so that we can give *more* to those who really need it."

Who wouldn't want to unify around a mission like that?

TWO

MANAGE TO THE ONE

Give the Man His Guitar

In 2016, Chester was preparing to deliver a keynote address in a sports arena to the 9,000 managers of Tesco, the U.K.'s largest grocery store chain. To say the company's planning committee was anxious would be an understatement. Hoping to make the session focused on galvanizing the business around the purpose and values, the organizers wanted everything to be perfect. Thus, they had gone through Chester's slides a half dozen times and revised and polished, but also scrubbed out a lot of the fun we try to inject into our presentations. Finally, the conference director, Karl James—a consultant who was hired to run the event—took the company organizers aside and kindly said to them, "Imagine that you bring Bruce Springsteen to town, but you tell him he can't play his guitar, can't sing his greatest hits, and can't let anyone dance on stage. You've hired Chester Elton for a reason; give the man his guitar."

The committee members chuckled, took a deep breath, and graciously conceded. That night as Chester stepped off stage, the lead organizer exclaimed, "Brilliant!" We tell this story not because Chester loves being compared to the Boss—he does, of course, but he's not delusional. He doesn't even play the guitar. The point: As leaders can enhance team performance by addressing generational differences between their team members, many of the best managers we've studied also see huge payoffs in team productivity by tailoring the management of their direct reports to tap their people's unique talents and motivations optimally and best developing each employee's career.

We call this managing to the one.

You'd be hard-pressed today to find a business person who doesn't recognize that personalization has become the gold standard for consumer products and services. Netflix probably knows your viewing preferences better than your significant other, with each of its 100 million subscribers offered a unique experience each time they log in. Pandora and Spotify have changed the way people listen to music by providing personalized radio stations. Google and Facebook make their billions by personalizing the ads shown to users. Well, it's time for personalization to be appreciated as the gold standard for managing people, for much the same reasons that personalization drives customer enthusiasm and loyalty. People want to have an authentic relationship with their managers, and be encouraged to pursue a handful of their particular passions.

Conventional wisdom has long been that all members of a team should be treated the same because that assures fair management. With all due respect: *Bwahaha!* That is old-school thinking, and it prevents leaders from optimizing the allocation of responsibilities among team members according to their particular motivations and abilities. It also means missing out on rewards that can be reaped by giving people opportunities to tackle challenges that they'll actually enjoy.

Now, we recognize telling a busy manager that he needs to consider the range of work styles and particular needs of each of his employees may seem like an undue burden. Frankly, it might irritate the you-know-what out of him. The better way to consider the challenge of team members' differences is as a golden opportunity to build a heterogeneous team, where people's various passions and skills add to the collective intelligence and productivity of the group.

Many leaders think about team diversity in fairly narrow terms: Gender, ethnicity, religion, sexual orientation, and age. But there's another kind of diversity that can be just as powerful: Differences in work styles, or the ways in which people think about, organize, and complete tasks. "When members of a team all have the same style, you'll quickly run into trouble," said Carson Tate, a productivity expert and the author of *Work Simply*. "For example, if everyone has a linear, analytical, and planned approach to work and dislike disruption, (then) innovative new product development would be impossible." In other words: *Somebody* needs to shake things up.

In a recent conversation with Greg Piper, worldwide director of continuous improvement at Becton, Dickinson & Co.—a 51,000 employee medical technology firm—he told us, "I don't want a bunch of people like me on my team, I want different skill sets, different ways of thinking. Now, admittedly, that can be a real pain for a leader. It means you have to work harder because not everyone thinks like you do, but you'll have a better team overall."

It's ironic that while personalization in customer offerings and services has been greatly facilitated by technological advances, technology has cut down on face-to-face time between managers and employees. So much communication that was once conducted in person is now done by file sharing, email, and project management programs. And while technology has given managers powerful ways to track and evaluate individual performance, it can't take the place of one-on-one conversations in discovering what drives people or, just as importantly, what is demotivating to them about their work.

The most frequent pushback about this topic, of course, revolves around time. How can a busy team leader possibly afford to tailor her management to each individual on her team? There is no question that managers are terribly pressed. And with the push for flatter management structures and more self-management by teams, not to mention leaders expected to produce their own deliverables as work groups have shrunk, the concept of spending more quality time with employees may seem to cut against the grain of prevailing practice. Well, meet John Pray. He is a retired US Air Force brigadier general and now president and CEO of Operation Homefront, a charity that helps military families thrive in the communities they have worked hard to protect. While generals aren't known as a warm and fuzzy bunch, Pray's leadership style is all about connecting with each individual on his team.

"I can't pay people what they may be worth in the private sector, so I have to find other ways to engage my team members," he told us. "My wife taught me that everyone has a story. By learning their story, I find out what they are proud of, and get an understanding of their aspirations. I have 120 people in my amazing organization, and while most of them work in other parts of the country, I work hard to find out what motivates them, how they hope to develop in their careers, what gives them a charge, and what frustrates them. This is not a one-time thing. It takes a long-term commitment to build the essential bonds of trust and confidence as we work together to help them grow."

If Pray can personalize his management of 120 people, doesn't it seem possible to do so with the smaller teams that most leaders oversee and interact with more directly?

Perhaps the most persuasive argument is that it costs so much more to recruit new talent—some estimates put it at as much as 150 percent of an employee's annual salary—than it does to develop existing employees. "Investing in talent development is vital for employers because it directly affects employee retention, motivation, engagement, and productivity," says Sarah Perez, director of the executive MBA programs at the University of North Carolina. "Millennial employees, in particular, are interested in learning and have indicated that they are likely to look elsewhere if their employers fail to give them opportunities to learn and acquire new skills."

The good news is that developing people doesn't have to take a huge bite out of a manager's time. Many team leaders use some form of the following best practices. They can be learned and are relatively painless to implement. The concepts are: job sculpting, replacing the performance review with the continuous review, and having frequent, brief aspirational conversations to review progress on development goals and discuss career issues. We'll address them in turn.

CRAFTING JOBS—ONE BY ONE

Good managers have been trying to find ways to make work more rewarding from time immemorial. As we meet with those kinds of leaders, many tell us it's just common sense to sit down with each of their people regularly and work on career development. After all, it's one of the few things they *do* control. It usually takes years to affect an employee's compensation in a meaningful way, and they can't give out better perks or benefits if an employee is rocking it (*I'm going to give you a better dental plan, Johnson; I've seen your kids and they're a mess*). No, what managers can do is help their people develop. As Eric Clayberg, a software engineer manager at Google, said: "Engineers hate being micromanaged on the technical side, but love being closely managed on the career side." Don't we all?

Now this practice has a name: We call it *job sculpting*.

What does it entail? It's the art of forging a customized career path to help employees do a little more of what they find motivating and little less of what frustrates them—increasing your chances of retaining and engaging talented people. While sometimes sculpting might involve substantial changes in responsibilities, and might even eventually mean facilitating a team member's move to a new role in another team, we've found that these cases are rare. Most often relatively small changes in responsibilities or work situations create huge boons in the productivity and loyalty of team members.

The simple but profound truth in job sculpting is that when people's jobs give them the opportunity to do more of the kinds of things that satisfy their key motivations, they are going to be happier and more engaged in their work. Seems logical, right? But there is a prevalent notion that if people are unhappy with their work it will take a Herculean effort to change things, that they might have to quit and find their dream job. For the vast majority of people, that's just nonsense. Most don't need to take a risky leap; they just need to make small changes in their work lives. The happiest people we've spoken with didn't find their bliss down a new path; they made course corrections on the path they were already on. And managers play a key role in this process.

Jose Maria Zas is American Express's president of global card services for Argentina, Brazil, Mexico, and Latin America. He told us, "The best results I achieve is when I take the time to create individual 'profiles' of each team member, including their professional strengths and development opportunities along with their personal motivations. I get to know not only their career goals but their life goals. Using this analysis, I can then build teams that will complement and drive one another."

Some further wisdom comes from James Waldroop, who served as co-director of the MBA Career Development Program at Harvard Business School for 19 years, and Timothy Butler, who is the program's current director. They have found that Harvard MBAs they place into jobs are more likely to stay and stay committed if the work matches more of their deeply embedded life interests. These are not hobbies or personal interests, but their work passions. "Deeply embedded life interests do not determine what people are good at—they drive what kinds of activities make them happy. At work, that happiness often translates into commitment. It keeps people engaged, and it keeps them from quitting," they said.

These two PhDs argue that leaders can gain a competitive advantage through this process—not only in retaining and engaging talent, but in making it clear during recruiting that personal development is a priority in their workplaces. For instance, Waldroop and Butler have noticed that firms recruiting their students have a significant advantage over competitors when they emphasize a commitment to helping their professionals think about and manage their careers—a fact that many of their MBAs cite as key in choosing one firm over another.

But then, of course, managers must deliver on the promise. How?

That takes a little persistence and a touch of resourcefulness. For instance, a salesperson with a passion for quantitative analysis might be given a stretch assignment to work with market research, while still selling. An engineer who yearns to be more creative might help the communication team design new sales support materials or user manuals—again, while retaining her primary role in engineering.

John Lowery, CEO of the 300 person Michigan firm Applied Imaging, says this process means paying attention to the little things you hear from your people: "We have a technical specialist who loves photography, so we've asked him to take pictures at our corporate events. He brings every bit of equipment imaginable and is so engaged. We have a woman on our front desk who is an English major. We asked if she would mind proofing our company brochures before we go to print. She said: 'I'd love to do that.' She's given us great feedback, and does she ever feel valued!"

Harvard's Waldroop and Butler cite the example of Carolyn, a star analyst they met at a leading Wall Street firm, who was talented at designing sophisticated quantitative approaches. Executives tried to ensure Carolyn's loyalty by giving her above-average raises and bonuses, but unbeknownst to them, she was thinking of leaving. Although she enjoyed the analysis and math in her work, she wanted to have more of an impact on decision making and group direction—a say in who the group hired, how the team was structured, and how they could interact better with other areas of the company. In short, she was motivated by developing others and being in charge (what we call *ownership*).

The story does have a happy ending. Carolyn and her boss sat down and arrived at a player-coach role for her as coordinator of research. She continued to do her work as an analyst, but also assumed a leadership role on a couple of cross-functional teams. They got her involved in hiring and promotion decisions, and she was asked to sit in when the executive team brainstormed on strategic direction. A year later, leaders said the research group had never been more productive, and Carolyn was happy and engaged.

It must be said that this kind of tailoring approach involves people doing things that you actually need done, not just those they would *like* to do more of. Just because an employee enjoys doing an activity doesn't mean they *should* do more of it or that your team *needs* more of it done. In some cases, we also must accept that the person might not be *good* at what they love to do. The activity must be not only motivating but also a strength for the person, or something they can realistically get better at with time and effort. Work is not simply about people pursuing passions. If it were, we would have a surfeit of professional chocolate tasters and secret agents. No matter how hard the two of us try, we'll never play professional hockey or win *The Voice*. Things we are passionate about, but not very good at, are what we call hobbies.

So, how can managers tailor jobs to optimize a bit more of their people's enthusiasm and talents, all within the boundaries of what's best for the team and its performance mandates?

Dan Helfrich of Deloitte asks his people: "What do you want to get better at?" to help determine their core motivators. "I want to know about a challenge they feel ready to take on, but haven't been given the chance to do in another team. Then as the time goes along, wow, the alignment that comes from giving them small tasks or opportunities that align with what they shared with you."

Helfrich gave us the following example: One of his team members was the hub of coordination for multiple work streams. The woman knew the status of everything that was going on in the team. "But," he said, "she shared that she was starting to feel like a reporting mechanism; she wasn't being given a chance to think creatively or strategically. She had this skill set as a conductor that was highly regarded, but it felt limiting to her." So Helfrich assigned the woman to take the lead on a new project, allowing her to work with a blank white board and lead the creative process as opposed to taking other people's white boards and making sense of them. "That has unlocked career growth that wouldn't have happened otherwise," he added.

We present below a few more questions that can help in this process in an informal way. This is by no means an exhaustive list, but a few thought-starters to ask each employee:

List the activities you look forward to doing most at work:

_____

_____

_____

What is it about these activities that energizes you?

_____

_____

_____

List the activities that frustrate you:

_____

_____

What is it about these activities that demotivates you?

_____

_____

_____

If you had three wishes for your career, what would they be?

_____

_____

_____

Those are simple questions, admittedly, but a starting point to find out what motivates your people. Another way to do this is by using an assessment, commonly (and rather unfortunately) called a "personality test." The best-known of these is probably the Myers-Briggs Type Indicator, developed by two enterprising housewives during World War II to align women who were entering the workforce with jobs that suited their personalities. Later, psychologist Robert Hogan developed his own way to help leaders understand the personalities of those they employ and how individuals approach problem solving and difficult situations. DiSC—based on the work of psychologist William Moulton Marston—provides a personality profiling system that centers on the behavioral traits of dominance, inducement, submission, and compliance. There are also several popular tests that determine teammates' strengths, including StrengthsFinder and CoreStrengths. And there are some good assessments out there to improve a team's ability to recognize their own and others emotions, such as those found in *Emotional Intelligence 2.0*.

If you've moved jobs in the past few years, chances are you've filled one of these out—maybe holding your breath hoping your results would be considered *normal*, so that the company wouldn't rescind its offer. Some 60 to 70 percent of new hires now report taking some form of assessment before coming on board with their organizations.

Many of our clients use these tools, and they've seen real benefits from implementing them. What's interesting, however, is how passionate and definitive some organizations become about the certain assessment they use, as if it's the only *true* assessment. That's not a knock on any particular tool. Managers can benefit greatly from having their team members engage in any of them; nor are we suggesting that leaders subject their people to dozens of these tests. Heavens no. Our point is that each of these instruments measures different things. Personality tests measure who people are at their core and how they might behave in various situations, strengths' tests measure natural talents, emotional intelligence tests determine how well people understand and empathize with others.

We entered the world of assessments a few years ago when we noticed that there was no scientific way to identify what *motivates* people, or what doesn't motivate them. In short, we didn't know how to help our clients understand what gets their people excited about their work and what makes them drag their feet.

We started helping managers job sculpt after we developed the Motivators Assessment. We found it provided a way to diagnose how each team member's specific tasks are (or are not) aligned with his or her motivations, and helped team leaders uncover often-minor changes that could lead to improvements in morale and results. An added benefit, which we hadn't expected, is that when assessments are shared with others on the team, they can help teammates understand causes of friction and improve their working relationships. Understanding differences in people's core drivers allows employees to *get* one another in a much more thoughtful manner, and thereby work more collaboratively and empathetically.

With that said, we would never claim that the Motivators Assessment is the one-and-only test a team will ever need, it's simply a tool that helps measure something that hadn't been measured before—what people *love* to do.

We discussed in chapter 1 the roll-up of the results of the tens of thousands of Motivators Assessments that people have completed, and how they broke down by generational groups. Considering them individually, we have found that each person has what we could call a *motivation fingerprint*, a unique combination of the twenty-three motivators. Some might be driven most by team-work and challenge, others more by learning and service, and still others by helping colleagues to develop their talents. Some people thrive on recognition, while others feel awkward when singled out for a public commendation. Some are driven strongly by the desire to make a lot of money, while others thrive much more on excite-ment and creativity. Some folks need more coaching, while others will find such help to be cloying.

When team members and their managers have a more refined understanding of all the various motivation profiles on a team, they can work together to sort out some changes in the alloca-tion of tasks and hopefully provide members with new opportuni-ties to pursue their individual passions a bit more often. They can also become more empathetic to one another's work styles, which helps people work in better harmony.

Let us describe how this process can be conducted by using the case of a marketing team we worked with. We've changed the team members' names to keep them confidential, but in the graph on the next page we've plotted the Motivation Assessment results of three of the employees of the larger team. We've selected this triumvirate not only because each of their jobs was eventually sculpted to better suit their motivations, but because they had been having trouble working with one another. Let's meet Mo-nique, Craig, and Erin on the next page.

In a meeting with this team, we presented everyone with a graph like this one (just with the entire team on it), which showed everyone's top and bottom motivators. We gave them some time to digest it, then asked for them to look for the top seven motiva-tors they shared in common with others. These are the *similarities*.

		MONIQUE	CRAIG	ERIN
TOP 7 MOTIVATORS	1.	Friendship	Variety	Creativity
	2.	Service	Impact	Family
	3.	Variety	Learning	Learning
	4.	Fun	Service	Autonomy
	5.	Empathy	Excelling	Money
	6.	Impact	Family	Ownership
	7.	Teamwork	Problem Solving	Variety
BOTTOM 3 MOTIVATORS	21.	Prestige	Developing Others	Teamwork
	22.	Social Responsibility	Fun	Empathy
	23.	Money	Money	Social Responsibility

In this case, you'll note that variety pops up in each of the three individuals we are looking at. The leader could see these results and realize that to keep this group motivated, she needs to throw a few diverse assignments into the mix now and then. That was a good macro learning.

Next, we asked the team to look for the motivators in their top seven that were particular to each person, which we call *uniques*. For example, the group noted that Monique was the only one who had friendship, fun, and empathy in her top seven. And, indeed, Monique and the team readily agreed that she was driven by these concepts. Now, if we were the managers of this group, and we had to send someone to a networking event to build relationships, who would we pick? Obviously it would make a lot of sense to ask Monique. Chances are she would return with some great leads to build our business, and would be enthusiastic in doing it.

The group then turned to Craig's results. His unique motivators were excelling and problem-solving. Indeed, Craig and the team heartily confirmed that appraisal. So, with that said, as managers who would we ask to tackle the next tough customer issue? Craig, of course would be ideal. And, the team was unanimous that there was no one more enthused at follow up or taking on a challenge.

So, that left Erin. Her uniques were creativity, autonomy, money, and ownership. We asked who the group would assign to come up with the next big idea, and they all agreed it would be Erin, no question. Give her a sense of ownership, some time, a little space, and watch what happens.

We next instructed the team to examine what we call *cautions*, by which we mean red flags about how people's motivators might cause problems regarding tasks assigned or how the team functions. Are there sources of friction between team members due to differences in their profiles, perhaps because a motivator is high for one person and low for another? With this three, the discussion became intense.

As an aside, one of the discoveries that came out of this was the plan Craig's manager had for his career was not ideal. Craig was being groomed to replace the manager if she got promoted or moved to another role (which was not uncommon for people at her level). The problem was that developing others was low on Craig's list of motivators, coming in third from last. We asked his manager in a private meeting later whether Craig actually *liked* managing people. The boss hesitated. She didn't know. We brought Craig into the conversation. He knew he was in line for the manager's job. Money might have been his last motivator, but he wasn't about to say no to more of it. And, he assumed, a promotion was the natural path of progression. When pushed, however, he admitted managing people was draining, frustrating even. As we asked him to describe his *worst* days on the job, the tasks he was most often involved with were mentoring younger employees about their roles in his projects and working one of his project teams through sticky personnel issues and conflicts. Those were bad days. But when we asked about his *best* days, he brightened up. That was easy. On those days he was usually offsite working with clients, solving their issues, and looking like a hero. He loved to do those things, and he was good at them.

So, could Craig be a good manager? Perhaps. He might be *able* to do it. But, we told his current manager, there was a good chance Craig could be miserable, which might lead to burnout. It also might be clear, pretty fast, to his employees that his heart wasn't in the role. So, as we sat with Craig and the manager, we asked if it would be possible for him to continue as an independent contributor (where he was doing a terrific job) but still grow in his career? Could he take on other tasks, broaden his reach, assume more responsibility, earn more money, and not manage others? After some back-and-forth and early hesitation, the manager acknowledged that it might be possible, after all, if Craig could grow his role. One idea, perhaps, might be to assume some of the social-media assignments that were currently being outsourced to contractors. That would mean learning new skills (which Craig was eager to do; learning is number three on his list). During the discussion, Craig could not have been more engaged. Ideas started to flow, and soon a few commitments had been made. At that point the two were still in a fact-finding phase, exploring ideas and brainstorming, but this employee felt that he'd been listened to, and the manager was willing to research options because she knew there could be a benefit for her team and the overall organization.

A few months later, when we checked back, Craig's skill set had started to expand and he and his manager had had a few more energizing career discussions. In time, the supervisor felt confident his responsibilities and salary could increase as he grows.

Coming back to the larger group meeting, other cautions the team uncovered about themselves helped Erin, Craig, and Monique understand why they hadn't been getting along. They all respected each other's work, but each found the others exasperating at times. They hadn't, however, been able to articulate exactly *why*. Their assessment results suddenly made the reasons for the problems clear.

The first thing they made note of was that while "fun" was a high motivator for Monique, coming in at number four, it was second from last, at number twenty-two, for Craig. The two realized that this had been a source of some irritation between them. They would be in meetings and Monique would be cracking jokes, telling stories, and asking about people's lives outside of work (friendship is number one for her, after all, and empathy is number five). However, all the time she was being fun, sociable, and empathetic, Craig would be tapping his fingers on the conference room table. *Can we get back to work yet?*

As we visited with those two in our follow-up meeting a few

months later, their relationship had improved. In coming to understand Craig's motivators, Monique realized that when she's in
a meeting with him, she needs to be more focused on the tasks at
hand or he'll get frustrated. As for Craig, he told us he truly does
want Monique involved in his projects—she knows everyone and
has tons of ideas—so he'd begun to build in time to relax and let
down his hair. That way, she'll be more engaged. These simple
understandings helped the situation considerably. They may never
end up BFFs, but they now understand each other and accept
that they each bring diverse but important motivations and skills
to the team.

One last caution discussed was regarding the motivator of
money. Erin had ranked it as number five. We told her and the
team that wasn't bad, not at all. In turn, she shared her background: Growing up in humble circumstances, money meant security. Perhaps that was why, others noted, she was the one on the
team who fretted about every penny that went out the door.

That grabbed our attention: Money was a big motivator for
Erin, but the team wasn't using it.

Since Craig ran a lot of projects, he had been managing much
of the budget; and frankly, the team was spending cash like a Bev-
erly Hills teen with mom's credit card. Take another look at Craig's
motivators, and you'll see money was dead last. It's not that Craig
didn't like money, or want more of it, but he didn't *get* money. We
don't mean to be cruel, and suggest that Craig was clueless. On the
contrary, he was a bright guy. It's just money was not something
he spent much time worrying about. In his personal life, he told
us, his wife balanced their checkbook and did their taxes. When
we discussed in our offline meeting with his director the notion

of growing in his career without the need to manage people, he had only a vague notion of how much money he made annually. Perhaps most germane for this discussion, Craig had no real notion of how much was left in the team budget at any given time, let alone something more complex—like if the team made a profit on each project.

In short, he probably wasn't the guy to take care of the budget.

You'll notice that money was also a dead-last motivator for Monique. When we asked the group if she might be suited to handle budgeting, exactly no one thought that was a good idea. Friendship was such a huge motivator that she typically wanted to use people she knew for outside projects—cost be damned. Monique chuckled and sheepishly nodded in agreement. She didn't want the assignment anyway. It held no allure.

So, eventually, the team turned to Erin. It seemed so obvious at this point. As they talked about it, they realized if Erin was given this task she'd watch every expenditure like the money was her own, get multiple bids on projects to ensure the best price, and make sure they stayed on budget with every line item. Indeed, in checking later, spending had already been curtailed. As for Craig, he now had more time to focus on what he loved to do—serve clients—and Erin felt like she was making an important contribution to the success of the team.

Admittedly, we have just made the process of team improvement sound simple. Honestly, it was in this case. These three were uber-smart, open to learn, and eager to change to advance the team and themselves. Many groups, unfortunately, can be more resistant. But, as Theodore Roosevelt once said, "The best thing you can do is the right thing, the next best thing is the wrong thing, and the worst thing you can do is nothing." In short, you must try.

We have found a diagnostic process like this can be remarkably empowering for all sorts of teams. Not only does it help managers consider how to adjust their management to the motivations of their individual direct reports and what reassignments they might make, including new opportunities they could provide employees, it also helps team members take better charge of their own careers and put their fingers on the specific things that will help them be most engaged on the job. It certainly provides language that can make discussing possible changes with their bosses more focused.

A manager who benefitted from the process is Diane Weed, vice president of the Denver division of The Wendy's Company. When her third-grade teacher told her that she was a natural leader, she took that and ran with it. Today, Weed has eight direct reports who oversee all the restaurants and the thousands of Wendy's teammates in the Rocky Mountain area. She put her Motivators Assessment results along with her team members' on a grid (like the one we just saw) and examined the similarities, uniques, and cautions.

"I'm now able to reflect on how my motivators may impact others in positive and negative ways," she said. "For example, 'pressure' is a top motivator for me, I thrive on tight deadlines and an adrenaline rush, but I have a subordinate who has pressure as her last motivator. I now know to be sensitive to this as I interact with her if I want to get maximum performance. I've learned that she prefers more lead time to respond to requests. When I ask for things on a moment's notice, or increase my leadership tension on a particular 'ask,' it puts additional stress and pressure on her. She doesn't produce her best work."

In fact, when we met Weed's team, the team member who had pressure as a low motivator told us that single *aha* "saved my career."

Another eye-opener, added Weed, was that seven of her eight team members had 'learning' as a top driver, where for her it fell in the bottom three. "I have had to be more cognizant of that when I'm developing meeting agendas, personal development ideas, and so forth, to ensure I'm providing my people with opportunities to learn and grow," she said. "Now, I facilitate formal discussions around specific books and business articles, and I also incorporate time for the team to interact more casually with each other—providing them with a format to learn from each other's experiences. A positive outcome has been seeing the team evolve as individuals *and* business partners."

Whether we manage a team in fast-food or high-tech or healthcare, we have to acknowledge our most important assets can walk out the door at any moment and begin working for a competitor. To retain good people, we must learn what drives them, and undertake the task of sculpting jobs to benefit both them and the organization.

THE PERFORMANCE REVIEW BECOMES THE CONTINUOUS REVIEW

Managing to the one is not only about addressing individual team member's passions in their daily work, it's also about assessing each person's job performance and helping improve it through ongoing conversations. Research has shown that teams perform better when every member is confident that the people around them are competent and working at a high level. Makes sense. And that confidence is bolstered when teammates know that the performance of all team members is being carefully evaluated. As Richard Clark, a University of Southern California professor, says, "When people doubt that one or more of their team members are competent, and when they believe that the capabilities of the other members are necessary to get the job done, motivation suffers dramatically." Clark's findings are backed up by the Google Project Aristotle study, which found a core factor in the highest-performing teams was that members trusted one another to deliver on promises and get their jobs done.

We find a demotivation effect happens when employees don't have each other's backs. If one team member (or several) are not performing well, that generally means others have to pick up the slack, and the overall team performance can suffer. That hurts things like team reputation with other work groups and their leaders, as well as tangible results such as limiting bonus amounts and raises. Who wouldn't find such outcomes dispiriting? And what manager would want her team members to be fine with that kind of situation? That's why the best team leaders are rigorously attentive to individual performance issues and make corrections quickly by thoughtfully assessing the sources of the problem and closely guiding improvement in a caring and compassionate but efficient manner.

Greg Piper of Becton, Dickinson & Co., holds one-on-one performance review sessions every other week for thirty minutes with his team—even though all his people are remote, spread throughout the United States, Mexico, and the United Kingdom. "'What do you want to talk about?' is always the first question I ask," said Piper.

One amazing bit of data about the value of such frequent check-ins comes from performance management firm Better-Works. Research the firm conducted found employees who meet and discuss progress toward goals with their managers *weekly* are up to twenty-four times more likely to achieve their goals. Think about how extraordinary that finding is. Even if you saw a fraction of that improvement, the return on the investment of your time would be impressive. Let's say, for kicks, that the researchers got their math wrong by a factor of ten. Weekly checked-on employees would still be more than twice as likely to hit their goals, and isn't that a good enough reason to enhance the frequency of your one-on-ones with each person on your team?

If managers don't take this proactive approach, the effects on team morale, and hence on performance over time, are almost always corrosive. People tend to gripe about others, and resentments can fester into dysfunctional team relations. Some even consciously slack off on their own work since others seem to be getting away with it. Clark advises that, for these reasons, "A crucial support for team motivation is to inform team members that the organization will assess the individual contributions of each member of every team rather than only assessing the achievement of the entire team." And that means utilizing the standard procedure for evaluating individual performance: The annual performance review. Right?

When applied well, formal reviews did help foster employee development in the past. But much depended on the spirit with which they were conducted and how constructive and well-founded the appraisals of employees' performance were. The goal of offering people feedback and setting forth specific action steps for them to take in the coming year is unquestionably laudable. If the process is used to identify ways in which employees can develop their skills and experiences to help them progress, then we could not be more supportive of that mission. But, and there's a big but, there are many problems with the practice, and in recent years, it has fallen under a good deal of criticism. Many prominent firms including GE, Adobe, Microsoft, Price Waterhouse Cooper, the Gap, Accenture, Deloitte, and Netflix, to name just a few, have decided to either substantially alter the annual performance review or to abandon the practice entirely—replacing it with other processes for evaluating and developing employees that are more timely, frequent, and in the control of the immediate supervisor.

We call this *the continuous review.*

The biggest reason for the change: In today's fast-moving business environment, a yearly (or half-yearly, for that matter) appraisal is simply not responsive enough to address changes that teams are facing and help people respond. To navigate the volatile, uncertain, complex, and ambiguous world, people need much more regular feedback and guidance—especially younger workers who are unwilling to wait an entire year to learn about their strengths or needed-improvement areas.

The performance appraisal process is not only too infrequent but often poorly executed. How many of us, both evaluators and the evaluated, haven't seen that it can have adverse effects? One expert on the appraisal process, University of Chicago Professor Kevin Murphy, claims that reviews are often a source of anxiety and annoyance rather than a font of useful information. Wharton Professor Peter Cappelli makes a thoughtful observation about how the feedback in these reviews, even if it is fair and balanced, is often received badly by employees, pointing out, "Humans are hard-wired to focus on the negative. So 'balanced' feedback always leaves us concentrating on the bad parts." HR people can be critical too. A survey conducted by Sibson Consulting found that of HR executives surveyed, 58 percent gave their own organization's performance review systems a C grade or lower.

Fast Company offered a particularly damning assessment of the process, quoting Laszlo Bock, senior vice president of People Operations at Google, who made no bones that the annual review is, "a rule-based, bureaucratic process, existing as an end in itself rather than actually shaping performance. Employees hate it. Managers hate it. Even HR departments hate it." The final word is for UCLA researcher Samuel Culbert, who wrote a book about getting rid of the performance review process. He calls it "a curse on corporate America."

Of course, if your company conducts these annual or semiannual reviews, you don't have the option of simply jettisoning the process. What you can do is to make them as constructive as possible, but more importantly implement your own frequent, one-on-one continuous review meetings with your team members in which you discuss their job performance and assignments weekly.

In addition, we also recommend other regular meetings to discuss each person's career development goals. These get-togethers should feel more fluid and less formal—evoking less anxiety—but in reality are quite tightly structured.

ASPIRATIONAL CONVERSATIONS

Aspirational conversations are brief but regular career meetings with members of a team. We realize that the notion of conducting such conversations with each person on your team may feel like an enormous time drain. That can happen if the meetings aren't structured or focused. First, understand they don't have to be long. Most managers have them last from fifteen to thirty minutes, tops—depending on the needs of the person. If a serious issue arises, they might take a little longer, but that should be rare as these aren't supposed to be disciplinary, project update, or planning meetings. It's the one meeting you'll have that has the sole object of building an employee's career—and what employee wouldn't come to that meeting engaged?

Generally, we've found it's best to hold these aspirational conversations once a month with direct reports and once or twice a year with skip-level employees—those people who work for the managers who work for you. In some high turnover industries, such as retail, hospitality, food service, customer service, or healthcare, our experience has found holding them as often as weekly with direct reports can cut turnover dramatically.

Aspirational conversations are not about gauging day-to-day performance and hitting goals; they are focused on career development, providing regular opportunities for you to listen to employees' ambitions to learn and grow and to counsel them about their progress forward. Calling them aspirational conversations (or something like that) helps to impress on employees that the purpose in the meetings is not to look over their shoulder to micromanage or criticize day-to-day behaviors, but to get out of the daily grind and help them look into the future, stretch a little, and craft a path for their personal progress.

This meeting is neither for reward or punishment. Rather, it's a process to facilitate methodical individual development. While you may have no choice but to assign grades in a performance review, in these conversations you can raise issues without employees fearing you're tallying a score that will be held against them. When such career meetings are conducted in a spirit of true conversation—of give and take and exploration—we find that people also tend to open up much more about their struggles, motivations, sources of frustration, and problems they see in how the team is operating. It's worth noting that while we've seen this practice be greatly appreciated by employees at all levels, it is likely to be especially fruitful in motivating and developing your Millennial team members.

One of the inspiring leaders we've discussed this practice with is California Pizza Kitchen CEO G.J. Hart, who told us, "What differentiates our company's best leaders is that they focus on helping each team member exceed their own expectations." As part of this process, Hart counsels his GMs and other managers to listen carefully and seek to understand why things are the way they are in their employees' worlds—their challenges as well as their career goals. As such, he advocates managers, "have conversations with their people about the way forward and what that might look like." Sometimes, he notes, these conversations will help a manager make course corrections if an employee has unrealistic expectations that might lead to frustration. "Managers can help team members understand why it might not be possible to get everything they want right now," he said.

On the flip side, career conversations with teammates can help identify obstacles that managers can remove. Hart said, "An important step is to think about if there are things that have held the individuals back so they can release the shackles, so to speak. When I came to CPK, it was very important to me that we encourage our people to dream big and enable them to make a difference in their roles. Our head of culinary had been here twenty years and had helped define the menu. We empowered him to pursue his individual passion for culinary inspiration and innovation, and it was so motivating to him. It's amazing what came out of that." What did emerge was an entire reimagining of CPK's menu including a renewed commitment to artisan pizzas made with hand-tossed, hand-stretched dough; new unique center-of-the-plate features including halibut and steak; and hand-crafted cocktails made with fresh seasonal ingredients. All of that has helped turn CPK into a restaurant that's hip again for sophisticated foodies, much more fun for employees to work at, and thriving for stakeholders.

CLARIFYING THE GAME PLAN

To ensure that the constructive spirit of these career-focused meetings is understood by employees, and that each aspirational conversation is as productive as possible, it's vital to discuss the intent of the process and set ground rules as early as day one. In the first of these meetings, let employees know you'll be taking a balanced approach—attending to their career development *and* the team/organization's needs. Managers should also emphasize that while they'll actively engage with the employee in this development process, ultimately the employee is accountable for his or her personal growth and career planning. Accordingly, they should be aware that in these conversations they are expected to share their aspirations openly. And, at all times, they should be seeking opportunities and resources they believe could help them develop. As such, they should be on a constant lookout for growth—not just waiting for their manager to propose ideas.

As for the manager, she commits to helping her employees find training opportunities that make sense, assignments that can help her people stretch, and connections with others around the organization who can help expanded networks. She'll also provide a sense of the future direction of the organization and help identify opportunities for the type of skills that might be needed in the future. And, as time goes on, she monitors if anything has changed about the employee's vision for his or her career.

It's important to clearly explain that these conversations are going to be a forum for ongoing feedback, which means things might get a little uncomfortable now and then as development issues are covered that might be tough to hear. A manager must let the employee know that she will always raise such matters in a spirit of a constructive discussion and problem-solving. Letting the employee know up-front that he must be receptive to the bad as well as the good helps to calibrate expectations and build trust about the whole experience.

Susan Reilly Salgado, managing partner of Hospitality Quotient, said, "In my first meeting with a fantastic boss, many years ago, his first question to me was: 'How do you like to receive feedback?' His question allowed me to shape a fundamental aspect of our interactions based on what I felt would work best for me, and it opened a line of communication that allowed me to reveal myself—to share my preferences and insecurities. From that point forward, receiving his feedback was a breeze for me, and for him, and over time I was even able to ask him, 'How do *you* like to receive feedback?' We built a foundation of trust that has been the cornerstone of our relationship to this day."

Now, if an employee's skin is thin—and that's not uncommon—then the process might look and feel a little less direct and take a little longer. That doesn't mean the person can't progress in his or her career, it just means a manager may have to take more care—learning, for instance, what the person's sensitivity triggers are. But no matter how thick- or thin-skinned employees are, it still helps to be empathic when delivering hard-to-hear feedback to anyone. Offering up a few simple encouraging words such as, "I can imagine that you are feeling a little frustrated to hear me say that. Is that right?" can go a long way to help alleviate tension. More importantly, a manager should encourage the employee to become a participant in solving an issue by asking questions such as, "What ideas do you have on this area?"

Lastly, after a challenging development session, we've found two final questions can have a profound impact. They are: "Do you believe I've treated you *unfairly* in any way today?" and "Have I said anything that would make you feel I don't value you as an important part of the team?" If the employee says you have, then you have a chance to address the situation before it festers.

FLUID AND TIMELY DOESN'T MEAN FREEWHEELING

To ensure aspirational conversations stay on track, we advise establishing a simple structure and a fixed day, such as the first Tuesday of each month. Of course, a manager can craft these meetings in their own way, but we've found that a good basic format is to:

PREPARE BEFOREHAND. The day before, email the employee a quick list of things you think you should cover, then ask what they'd like to discuss. Also, review your notes from last time so you don't spend the first five or ten minutes getting up to speed and looking clueless—and worse, looking like you don't care about what's important to them. And remember that cancelling these meetings regularly undermines their usefulness and can disenfranchise employees.

MEET WHERE THEY PREFER. It's their career meeting, not yours, so ask if they prefer getting a soda or coffee in the cafeteria, going for a walk, meeting in your office or theirs, or in a conference room. Just don't do after-hours drinks. Do, however, meet in person whenever possible. If an employee is remote, use a video chat, not a phone call.

SET EXPECTATIONS. If you are just starting up these types of meetings and aren't clear about the purpose, then some of your people might assume the worst (i.e., I'm going to be disciplined). Let them know this is about their career and where they want to go. If you've met before, in the first few minutes quickly recap what you discussed in the last meeting, and then together set a brief agenda for your time. Make sure the meeting feels nonthreatening and positive. If you need to discipline an employee, set up a time separate from this conversation to discuss those issues.

USE AN INDIVIDUAL DEVELOPMENT PLAN. Have a roadmap to follow. These don't have to be fancy, with pie charts and bar graphs, just one page to help you keep track of each employee's goals and what development projects they have going on. (We'll discuss these more in a few pages.) As you work through their goals and opportunities, start with near-term, then work your way to the longer horizon.

TALK LESS. If you end up monologuing about anything, then this is your meeting, not theirs. You should be asking questions, helping craft realistic career expectations, and providing brief guidance. You might have to draw out the discussion with quiet employees, but the aim is for them to open-up and feel heeded, not lectured to.

ELIMINATE INTERRUPTIONS. Make your employees feel you are giving your undivided attention for the entire meeting. That means closing your door and turning off your phone. An actor friend told us about a scene he did with the great Anthony Hopkins. The most remarkable thing about Hopkins, he found, was the rapt attention he gave to anyone he was speaking with—from the lighting hands to the extras. If a director or producer tried to interrupt Hopkins, he would politely ask the interrupter to wait while he finished listening to the person he was engaged with. It was a terrific lesson in respect our friend never forgot.

DON'T END ON A NEGATIVE. Employees may still remember the constructive criticism (the bad) you've given during one of these meetings—it's human nature, after all—but if you book-end conversations with positives there's a better chance they'll still feel good coming out of it.

FOLLOW UP. Send a quick email about what was discussed, decisions made, and any constructive feedback that you asked them to consider. You might attach an updated individual development plan. Keep the note you send short and positive.

DEVELOP ME

It's possible, in this process, to lose sight of the forest of long-term career development and have these meetings become only about near-term goals and day-to-day work issues (the trees). That's not the intention here, and that's where an individual development plan (IDP) can help keep you focused on an employee's aspirations, while also linking progress to the goals of the team and larger organization.

IDPs don't have to be fancy. The best are usually only a page long and include:

Motivations/strengths the person would like to utilize more in their role:

_____

_____

Career goals and aspirations:

_____

_____

Skills, education, experiences, or assistance they will need to accomplish their goals:

_____

_____

2 or 3 development actions with due dates and people they'll need to involve:

_____

_____

A manager can print out each person's IDP beforehand and use it as a guide for discussion in each aspirational conversation. It can then be updated and emailed to the employee after each of these monthly get-togethers.

DON'T SKIP THE SKIP LEVELS

As for meetings with skip-level reports, here it's extra important to be clear why they are having a meeting with the potentially scary boss's boss. You'll want to focus on offering the person input about their professional development more than day-to-day assignments that you might not have as clear a picture about. You also typically won't offer as much constructive feedback as you might to a direct report, but more encouragement and ideas—as well as an overview of the direction of the organization to help them understand where their skills could be a benefit in the future. And, of course, the senior leader will actively listen.

It's important to make sure the employee's manager knows you are going to have the meeting, and to get a little feedback from that manager before your time together. A senior leader doesn't want to undermine the person's direct supervisor. We had a senior leader do this during a skip-level meeting with one of our direct reports back in our corporate days, and it was mostly our fault. During the meeting, our employee complained to the senior leader about a development plan we'd put in place for him, and the big boss said, "Well don't worry about that, remember you work for me, not Chester and Adrian." Sure, in theory we all worked for the senior leader, but we managed this guy day-to-day and his teammates were often frustrated because he didn't always deliver on his commitments. He also spent hours every day walking around schmoozing executives in their offices, which was the damnedest thing. We were trying to coach the employee, and had mistakenly kept it from the senior leader to not hurt the guy's reputation. We messed up in not disclosing the development plan, and then the big boss messed up giving the impression that the employee was immune from our direct supervision—which did not help the case either.

Now, with that stated, the positives of skip-levels certainly outweigh any potential negatives. In fact, the benefits of managing to the one in this way are so valuable that upper-level managers should strive to make the time for at least one or two direct meetings with skip-level reports annually. One manager we saw do this well is Catherine Cole, director of the American Express executive customer care group in Florida. She admits these meetings can be intimidating to some employees who likely have only infrequent contact with their boss's boss, so she asks a great set of questions to structure the conversations and make people comfortable opening up: Talk about your journey so far with American Express; Has your experience over the past year been beneficial to your growth and progress? What one or two things get you jazzed about coming to work every day? What makes you want to hit the snooze button? At the end of the meeting, she promises to follow up with anything they've raised that she might be able to help with.

Cole's employees (and her skip-levels) are among the lucky ones—those with a manager who takes the time to get to know their successes and their frustrations, who genuinely wants to develop careers and help her people grow. That's managing to the one at its best.

THREE

SPEED PRODUCTIVITY

Help New People and Teams Work Faster and Smarter

In an episode of *Seinfeld*, George Costanza interviews for a job. When the hiring manager says he's going out of town for a week and will make a decision when he returns, neurotic George is struck by one of his occasional jolts of overconfidence and decides to just show up while the fellow is away. The problem: George has no idea what his duties are and, when handed the "Penske File," does little but stuff it into an accordion folder. It doesn't end well.

As was typical on the show, George caused his own problems. But many people we speak with report dissatisfying experiences when joining teams. They are expected to get up to speed quickly, yet are often ill-informed about their responsibilities and are not introduced to the key people they'll be working with.

In a recent survey of new hires, only 39 percent reported that they believed they had a good understanding of what their job entailed after their first day, and three months later, only slightly more than half reported clarity about what was expected of them. Yikes. The same survey indicated that the most basic preparations for new teammates frequently are not attended to, with about one in five new people reporting they had no desk on their first day, a quarter saying they had no computer, and a third that they didn't get a phone. We talked with one newly hired midlevel manager who said she asked the executive she reports to if she could get a directory that listed staff by departments and roles, and he replied curtly, "Why would you need that?" Wow.

The effects of uncertainty are dramatic on turnover. Various attempts to quantify them estimate that the price of just one failed hire is between 100 percent and 300 percent of the employee's salary.

What new person doesn't arrive at a job believing they'll positively impact the quality of their new organization's products and services? Yet, by the end of six months, 86 percent of workers aren't even sure if they'll stay with their new companies, let alone positively impact anything. That's one big pendulum swing.

Fred Steckler, chief administrative officer of the U.S. Patent and Trademark Office, told us: "On the first day of work everyone is engaged; the job of the manager is to not mess that up!" Well said.

The challenge of successfully incorporating new team members is becoming even more acute with the increasingly intense productivity demands organizations face, not to mention the move toward more fluid teams. Conventional wisdom dictated that it took a year for new employees to learn the ropes, another year for them to break even, and, finally, in their third year they were supposed to be profitable. Obviously, that's outmoded. Today, we expect new people to learn all aspects of their jobs in about a month (sometimes less); pay for themselves by month two; and if they aren't productive and profitable in their third month we admit our mistake and "make them available to the market," as some folks in HR say.

Meanwhile, the problems of incorporating new team members aren't limited to those who are new to an organization. While in the past most teams stayed together for years, sometimes decades, the configuration of a team may now change several times within the same calendar year—with people flowing in and out. The benefits are in more optimal allocation of talent to drive faster innovation and meet workflow demands. But all this rapid-fire changing of team composition can lead to disruption. What team doesn't require some time to learn how to best work together? A striking example is airline cockpit crews. Today's pilots are superbly well-trained and follow strict protocols, which has made it possible to create extremely fluid teams who are usually brought together for just one flight. Pilots sometimes fly two or three aircraft with different crews in the same day. While this has allowed for fine-tuned allocation of crew assignments, there is a sobering side-effect: The National Transportation Safety Board has found 73 percent of flight incidents occur on a crew's first day of working together.

Okay, so is there any good news? There is plenty. In an extensive study of how employees can best be brought in to modern teams, conducted by Professor Keith Rollag of Babson College and his colleagues, the researchers revealed, "When comparing the experiences of rapid versus slow on-boarders, our study found that documentation and training were never the differentiating factors." In plain English, the academics discovered the most important things a manager could do with a new person on their team were spending time clarifying her role and building strong relationships with immediate team members and others around the company. Manager's soft disciplines, again, made the biggest difference.

This research and a number of other innovative studies have helped us identify the most important factors in successfully getting new people and new teams up to productivity faster. The solutions are simple enough that all team leaders can enact them; and, as we'll describe, we've seen many of these in action.

The three key factors to focus on are: security, context, and affiliation.

SECURITY: OVERCOMING THE FEAR FACTOR

If an employee is a new hire, or has been asked to relocate to your team from another work group, joining an established team can produce anxiety for both the new member and the team they are joining. Even the most confident can find themselves wondering: *Will the team be receptive to me, will my work be valued, will I be competent, will I be liked?* In turn, all too often, existing members of a team have questions of their own. They might display ambivalence or, worse, hostility toward a new member: Perhaps a friend left (or was let go) and the new member is taking that person's place. Maybe the new hire is seen as a threat, which is possible if she has experience or skills that others on the team don't. Bringing in a new team member may also slow down productivity for a while as the person gets up to speed. In short, when the composition of a team changes, it can become a petri dish of anxiety.

A lot of managers assume that the unease is just a symptom of newness, and that it's a natural condition that will take care of itself over time. Consider this, however: Dartmouth Professor Vijay Govindarajan, and the CEO of the Growth Leaders Network Hylke Faber, have found that managing successful transformational change—including team flux—has a lot to do with managing fear. Leaders need to ensure that people feel *secure* if a team is going to be successful. "When we're in the grip of our fears, we are at least twenty-five times less intelligent than we are at our best . . . (which is) when our more primitive, or 'crocodolian' brain wired for survival takes over," the researchers have written. "When our crocodiles are active, we are resistant to change and are operating from a fear of survival. Our crocodiles are trying to keep us safe, at the cost of innovation and change."

Typically, you bring in new people because you believe they're talented and can add to the dynamic of your group. You want them to fit the culture, but also to make things better. The last thing you need is for a new worker to feel inhibited about exercising her talents, but that's exactly how many people feel.

A number of practices can help enhance feelings of security.

A. Hire for culture fit

First off, bring the right people into your team. Let us tell you about Frank. When we met him on a business trip we wanted to hire him right away. We flew Frank to headquarters to interview with our staff, more of a formality really. We were shocked when the team didn't seem to want him. One team member, Scott, begged us not to hire the man. He had dug deeper into Frank's qualifications during his interview and the professed skills got thinner and thinner.

What did Scott know? We had spent much more time with Frank. We hired him.

Frank was a disaster, and it took us years to untangle ourselves from his influence. The lesson we learned: To ensure the best fit for existing team members *and* those new people coming in, listen to your team. Your first interview with a candidate is just a step, and your first impression *can* be wrong. Great leaders send candidates to meet the team, their boss, and one or two people in the organization who don't have a vested interest in the position. It's important to listen carefully; your subject matter experts, especially, can help you dig deeper.

In this process of aligning with culture, it's also important to ask candidates *why* questions. At some point in the interview your candidate is going to tell you a story about a difficult work situation they overcame. They'll sound like a champion from Greek mythology. To employ the Socratic Method, it's then vital to ask *why?* and then *why?* again to determine their real character and fit with your team. For instance, "Why did you take that direction over another?" "What would have happened if you'd gone the other way?" "Why did your value system make you do what you did just then?"

B. Begin orienting people before their start date

Often, there is an awkward and shocking disconnect for new team members between the love fest of the hiring process and their first day on the job. Assume, before they walk through the door, that their anxiety has begun to mount—*What's expected of me? How can I make a good impression?* One way to assure new people of your commitment is to begin the process of inculcation before they start. This can be as simple as sending, in advance, an old-fashioned, handwritten welcome letter to their home, along with any background on the organization and any paperwork they need to sign—which usually burns up a good part of their first day anyway.

To inform your team of who's coming onboard, send around an announcement about the person, clearly discuss why he or she was chosen over other candidates, and outline why the person's skill set is going to help the team succeed. For particularly critical roles, you might consider putting the new hire in touch with a few key staff members before they start, senior contributors who can help teach them about things in the trenches you might not even be aware of.

The value of starting early is perhaps most impressively demonstrated by the Netflix Culture Deck, a 124-page slide deck that employees review before joining that firm. The slides go through the nine behaviors the company values and offer up lots of clear and logical examples of how to live them. Despite the deck's length—seriously, it's 124 pages—in reality, it's a speedy read with only a few words per slide. The nine behaviors are uncomplicated concepts, like Selflessness and Honesty, and the examples are easy to apply, such as "Make time to help colleagues" and "Only say things about fellow employees you will say to their face." The deck has been downloaded more than 17 million times, and Facebook COO Sheryl Sandberg said that it, "May well be the most important document ever to come out of [Silicon] Valley." High praise.

It's hard to remember that Netflix, which now offers

Emmy-winning hits such as *Making a Murderer* and *Orange Is the New Black*, started out as a mail-order DVD house that was little more than a pesky dog nipping at the heels of industry giant Blockbuster and its 60,000 employees (a company whose stores have been converted into Cinnabons and Anytime Fitnesses). In its short life, Netflix has gone through several major transformations. So why write the slides and post them online for new people? Because articulating the culture helps initiate newbies before they walk through the front door; and with its rapid growth and development of new technologies, Netflix has had to bring onboard lots of new people, *fast*.

The articulation of the company's culture has been so effective in clarifying how employees are expected to behave that it has done away with many policies. For instance, there is no vacation or dress code policy (other than "we don't come to work naked"). The expense reimbursement process is five-words long: Act in Netflix's Best Interest.

C. Start early and see the big picture

When Melissa Aquino received a job offer to head up the Danaher Business System as vice president at corporate headquarters, she wanted to come in prepared. "Before I take any job, I want to know who are my stakeholders, and what does winning look like for them?" So she interviewed executives around the company and asked them three questions: What do you like about the team I'm joining right now, what does it do right? What do you *not* like? and What advice do you have for me? She summarized the findings for the CEO and his executive team, and put together a strategic plan with three key initiatives. "I was able to say here's what the team's stakeholders want, here's what winning looks like to them, and here's the strategy that could deliver it."

Doug Soo Hoo, former director of learning and development at Johnson & Johnson, explains that managers can encourage their new hires in this kind of process, and is "a good way to get out of 'sink or swim mode' and an investment in the company that also shows a caring for the success of the individual," he said.

D. Spend quality time on Day One

The most effective managers we've met understand that they need to spend a good amount of time with new people on their first day—personally greeting them, introducing them to their team, and showing them around. We've heard far too many stories of people who had little or no contact with their manager in their first week, let alone the first day.

When new sales associates join the Philadelphia 76ers, the first day is a really big deal. "If you looked at it from ten-thousand feet, you'd think it was pretty stupid," said Braden Moore, director of insights and analytics. "We gather the entire team and have the new person say where they are from, give a fun fact about themselves, then we make them run down a high-five tunnel and dunk a basketball (which is a Nerf Ball dunked on a six-foot hoop). We want you to put your guard down and learn to be comfortable being uncomfortable."

Added Jill Snodgrass, vice president of service and operations, "As managers, we coach our new people to make their fun fact really fun, to really bring it. Then in the Q&A our reps will ask the new people questions: What's your favorite meal? What would you rather fight: A horse-sized duck or one-hundred duck-sized horses. It's ridiculous stuff, but it gets people to loosen up and be vulnerable."

Part of any first-day conversation includes explicitly stating that you are strongly committed to helping them succeed. We loved how KimArie Yowell, senior director of talent development at Quicken Loans, explained how her leaders convey this commitment to each new person: "Our culture is unique—we're a loud, fun organization that hates corporate bureaucracy. This can be a shock to the system for some. Knowing that, our team leaders take time with each new hire, whether the person dives right in and embraces the culture off the bat or seems like they'll take a little time to warm up. Whether you've been with us ten years or ten minutes, we're committed to your success. You made a commitment to come and work with us, you've likely given up a lot, and we take that very seriously. You are now part of our family."

In addition to a formal Quicken Loans onboarding process, every team has developed its own new employee training program unique to its specific work. Developing feelings of collaboration and connection are top of mind; which means, if at all possible, new teammates are actually seated in the middle of the team or right by the leader, so they not only have instant access to support, but are literally surrounded by it.

E. Facilitate guidance from fellow team members

We're sure everyone who's started a job remembers vividly the discomfort of having to ask yet another question of a boss or colleague. *Oh, my gosh, I'm going back for the twelfth time today!* Some of us remember being snapped at with curt answers from those who had to get their own work done and didn't want yet another interruption from the new guy. This takes a concerted effort from team leaders, stressing to everyone on the team that questions are to be encouraged and answered fully, patiently, and *without* eye-rolling.

One of the best ways to assure that new people really feel free to ask all the questions is to assign a member of the team to be their guide. At the Massachusetts Institute of Technology, which employs 12,000 people in the Boston area, new hires are assigned a buddy who stops by the new employee's work area on their first day and introduces himself and make plans to have lunch together during that first week. The buddy's job is to show the employee around the larger MIT campus, make introductions into other departments, and be available to answer questions. Over the following months, they'll meet for coffee or a soda numerous times and invite the person to business and social events on campus. The buddy isn't expected to be a subject-matter expert, but a Jiminy Cricket who can offer experiential advice on succeeding in this fast-paced environment.

F. Articulate a team code of conduct

One of the trickiest issues in joining any work group is picking up on the team culture. One of the practices we've seen often recently is leaders' setting forth an explicit set of operating rules. These should not be laundry lists covering every possible positive idea. Seriously, Moses had ten and most people can't remember half. No, generally these are a simple set of three or four core concepts that include guidelines about how we interact with each other.

A terrific example was shared by Tanner Elton, head of

entertainment advertising sales for online retailer Amazon. He has a fast-growing team with twenty-five direct reports and another fifty support personnel—spread from Los Angeles, New York, Seattle, to Chicago. With the diversity of roles and locations, he and the managers who report to him spend extra time helping new hires understand what he calls the team's Rule of Three guiding principles.

Number one is No Excuses. "Because excuses, even when valid, are never impressive," the Amazon executive said. "We let them know we aren't a team culture that cares why things didn't work out, or why something won't work, but one that finds ways to solve for it."

Number two is Fail Forward. "That means we want you to take chances, be innovative, swing big, and if you fall on your face we'll celebrate it. We are going to cheer you for a fail because we will all learn from it, and it will lead us to eventual success."

Rule three is Do It. "That's built on the premise that we can sit in a room and ideate and brainstorm ways to improve the culture or close a deal, but we have to act, right now," Elton said. "Someone may tell me, 'You know who's amazing, it's John. He did such great work on that deal.' So I'll say, 'Tell him. Send a note to him before you forget. Right now. I'll wait.' We Act Now with everything to foster a sense of urgency."

Elton told us about a new account representative he hired who took these rules very much to heart. His Amazon team was still new and was only just starting to see some early success, but was also still having enough failures and frustrations to create some internal skepticism that this entertainment advertising thing would work. "The new woman came in and asked about the typical deal size," said Elton. "At the time, it was about $70,000 per theatrical release. But I told her deal sizes could be from $300,000 to $500,000 to a million plus, because they could be. Now, we'd never had a deal that big, but I didn't want to inhibit her."

With that in mind, the new hire started brainstorming creative ways to get those big wins. She came back with her first proposal soon after from a smaller studio to help release one of its new movies. "It's not as much as you usually do," she said. "It's only for $725,000." Elton was thrilled, and admitted that it was the largest deal his team had ever done.

"As soon as she demonstrated to the team what was possible—and she followed it up with other million dollar deals soon after—the entire team started believing in it," he said. "Now we've had multiple people deliver those kinds of deals."

Even if you don't want to set forth explicit ground rules for your team, we do suggest discussing in some detail the culture of your team with new members—or defining these together if a new team has just been formed. Every team has distinctive ways of operating and interacting that new people need to know about to feel secure. And there may be important ways that you would like new members to contribute to furthering the team culture.

CONTEXT: 'YOU ARE HERE'

Novelist Antoine de Saint-Exupery is quoted as saying: "If you want to build a ship, don't drum up people to collect wood and don't assign them tasks and work, but rather teach them to long for the endless immensity of the sea." This sage advice from the oft-quoted Frenchman speaks to the power of helping people appreciate the larger mission they are a part of, rather than just the minutia of their own role. And this is especially true with new employees or new teams.

One of the most powerful ways effective modern managers help people feel a sense of belonging is to help them understand full context—the importance of the work the team does and the specific contributions they are expected to make, as well providing a larger perspective of how this helps the overall business. These leaders also aid team members in understanding the real challenges the team and organization are facing, such as outside competition, and the goals the business is driving toward.

If culture is *who* we are as an organization or team and *how* we behave, context is *where* we fit in the world around us.

We'll come back to Netflix for a moment, which does a particularly good job of helping new teammates understand the company's place in the industry and the honest challenges they are seeing, during New Employee College. CEO Reed Hastings and all division heads explain every aspect of the businesses in great detail—helping newbies understand where each team fits into the grand puzzle.

The company's former chief talent officer Patty McCord (who is now a coach to other leaders) explained that Netflix instituted this college because employees needed to better understand the levers that drive their organization. "I recently visited a Texas startup whose employees were mostly engineers in their twenties. 'I bet half the people in this room have never read a P&L, I said to the CFO. He replied, 'It's true—they're not financially savvy or business savvy, and our biggest challenge is teaching them how the business works.' Even if you've hired people who want to perform well, you need to clearly communicate how the company makes money and what behaviors will drive its success."

For instance, at Netflix, McCord said, employees in the not-so-distant past were focused too heavily on subscriber growth, without awareness that expenses were running ahead of new money coming in. "We were spending huge amounts buying DVDs, setting up distribution centers, and ordering original programming, all before we'd collected a cent from our new subscribers," she added. "Our employees needed to learn that even though revenue was growing, managing expenses really mattered."

This concept of providing context seems so simple, but in practice many of us are so concerned with instructing employees on *how* to do their particular jobs that we give little time and attention to equally important context setting: *Why* the job needs to get done and for *whom* the work is being performed.

Pixar Animation Studios President Ed Catmull personally teaches the importance of context to all new hires, stressing that they must get the confidence to speak up and challenge the status quo. "I talk about the mistakes we've made and the lessons we've learned. My intent is to persuade them that we haven't gotten it all figured out and that we want everyone to question why we're doing something that doesn't seem to make sense to them. We do not want people to assume that because we are successful, everything we do is right."

Mobile payments company Square takes new hires to visit local merchants to understand how important their product is to those clients and exactly how it's used. Software firm Infusion runs a month-long boot camp for all new people, where it teaches every skill a person needs to know to do well at the company—from pitching new ideas and gathering requirements, to good programming practices and how to actually code.

For a manager, onboarding each new employee or new team should be considered a project. And in today's work environment, it's important to remember that this isn't just about teaching job skills, it's just as much it's about instilling an understanding of where the team fits in the big picture. Think of it as applying the red dot at the mall that says, "You are here."

AFFILIATION: THAT'S WHAT FRIENDS ARE FOR

The third key in facilitating speed-to-productivity is helping new team members build solid relationships with colleagues. Bonds like this create a stronger sense of affiliation—feelings of being accepted by one's coworkers, which, in turn, increase commitment to the team and organization.

We appreciate that the idea of helping your people develop friendships with their coworkers might seem a bit warm and fuzzy, even in a book on soft disciplines. We work closely with senior leaders, often CEOs, and we can count on the fingers of one hand the number who brought us in because they were worried about increasing *friendships* among their workers. So let us share some fascinating recent studies that have reinforced how vital it is to help today's new teammates develop relationships.

We mentioned earlier a study of business onboarding practices by Keith Rollag of Babson College and his colleagues. They found new teammates who were rapid on-boarders—those who got up and running quickly and most successfully—built a better network with a broader range of coworkers than most new people.

One of the companies in their study was a global energy firm. The researchers found that while most of the firm's new hires communicated regularly with only a few colleagues—mostly within their own teams—one new hire, Jake, "quickly become a central player." He established solid connections with many more members of the team and others outside his group, and became a valuable source of information, having tapped those he met effectively for what he needed.

The researchers highlight that some people, like Jake, are simply better at developing personal networks quickly, which might support the notion that this isn't a manager's job after all. Isn't it up to individual employees to step up and learn the skills of networking? The researchers argue that actually the lesson here is the reverse: Leaders who most successfully onboard people take what they call a *relational approach* to the task, actively assisting new team members in creating important social bonds.

Those findings were backed up by a remarkable study by Alex Pentland and a team at MIT's Human Dynamics Laboratory. They studied the communication patterns among high-performance teams versus lower performing ones, defining high-performance as those work groups "blessed with the energy, creativity, and shared commitment to far surpass other teams." And who wouldn't want a team like that? The professors studied a wide range of industries, giving team members electronic badges to wear that tracked communications. The results showed a distinctive pattern of chatter in the best teams, where all members were regularly in contact with one another. Inclusive-connectivity, they discovered, was the single most important factor in driving high-performance. It was "as significant as all the other factors—individual intelligence, personality, skill, and the substance of discussions—combined," the researchers wrote. And the longer it takes new team members to develop good, communicative relationships with their teammates, the longer the team's performance will be held back from its full potential.

We find that friendships at work foster not only stronger communication, but from the Gallup Organization's Q12 survey, the findings are pretty startling that having a best friend at work increases commitment to the company, trust in leadership, and overall engagement; while having multiple friends at work exponentially increases all the above. A separate survey found employees with at least six friends at work are twice as likely to trust management and are almost three times more likely to say they love working there (64 percent versus 24 percent on that last measure).

The antithesis of this is a team made up of loners, people who do not feel connected to those around them. When is that ever a good thing? Detached individuals are much more likely to be disconnected from their organization in every way measured.

Creating bonds of affiliation has typically been considered outside the bounds of a manager's job description. Seriously, when was the last time you were told to amp up the chumminess of your team? Yet consider the striking increase in team performance that MIT researchers noted at one bank call center that simply had everyone on the team go on coffee break together, versus the standard practice of staggering break times. Admittedly it was a pain for managers—having to redirect calls to other areas and cross-training other groups on their client needs to cover effectively—but something extraordinary happened that was well worth the extra effort. A key measure of the center's productivity—the average hold time for calls—dropped by more than 20 percent for teams that had been the lowest-performing and eight percent overall. Employee satisfaction scores also rose dramatically. Management was so impressed that this unassuming change could produce such dramatic results that the bank planned to change break schedules at all its ten call centers and anticipated increased revenue of $15 million due to productivity improvements. Admittedly, this is a case study of one center in one bank, but it does suggest that stronger social relationships within a team can help improve information flow as well as morale.

So how should managers go about helping their new hires or new teams foster these types of relationships faster? What follows are our Laws of Affiliation Building:

A. Assign new team members a task that *requires* them to meet others

When you bring a new person into your team, at least one early assignment should require the person to reach out to a good number of others on the team and around the organization. It might seem counterintuitive to give a newbie a wide-sweeping task, but creating a network is vital in bonding a person to the organization and getting up to speed faster, even though this particular task might take them longer to complete than an old-hand.

One vice president we spoke with does this to get her new hires off their islands, as she put it. She told us of one new manager who joined her team. "I have a very extroverted management style, but the new guy had a very introverted style," she said. The man's style seemed similar to another company executive, "So I sent him to spend a couple of days with that leader, shadowing him, sitting in his meetings, helping learn how that kind of leadership style could be really successful."

B. Arrange a Nonwork Outing for the Team

We saw the positive effects of creating bonding experiences in action in a big way when we were with G.J. Hart, CEO of California Pizza Kitchen. He had invited his leadership team of restaurant GMs—many of whom were new to the organization—to spend a full day giving back by repainting boys' and girls' clubs and rebuilding parks in a disadvantaged neighborhood during their annual operator's conference. When the team returned from their volunteer work, sweaty and dusty, they were arms slung around each other's shoulders and high-fives galore. It was a day they would never forget, and most we've spoken with since report that they created friendships that have lasted. They now feel that they can pick up the phone and get the support they need from a fellow GM, but more importantly from someone they think of as a friend.

Activities like this don't have to be complex, just something to get everyone talking and interacting. An outside lunch, a Frisbee toss in the park one afternoon, even getting the team together for bowling on a Friday afternoon can help bond people. As a manager, it's important for you to be particularly present at these outings—meaning you have to turn off your phone and focus on your people.

C. Facilitate sharing about one another's nonwork lives

Another great lever to create feelings of affiliation is for team members to become familiar with one another not only as colleagues, but as well-rounded individuals with common interests on the job and outside. Recall that Space Station Captain Chris Hadfield invited his team members to meet and share backstories about their lives before shooting out of orbit. By the time they were done getting to know each other, everyone understood where the others were coming from.

Dan Helfrich, leader of Deloitte's federal government services team, starts to create feelings of affiliation on teams he takes over by having them meet in person (even if they are all remote and have to travel), and they all share what they hope to accomplish with the team overall and for themselves as individuals. "It creates an environment where people get to know each other quickly in a trusting way and assimilate, and as a leader you start to put together this mosaic of people's interests and beliefs in why the work we are doing is important."

D. Take advantage of technology to inspire social bonding

The teams we've studied are increasingly building online spaces for employees to share updates, memories, and day-to-day happenings. These team forums or social newsfeeds not only help employees stay in touch more easily, but can also be used to crowdsource ideas, congratulate one another on achievements, and make special personal announcements.

The technology team at TED (you know their TED-talks) is spread over multiple U.S. states, so members use a lot of collaboration tools and videoconferencing. Investing in high-quality headsets for every team member makes a big difference, they say, as does insisting that each person find a room with a door they can close for privacy during online meetings. Some interesting traditions have developed on these video calls, for instance everyone wears a silly hat of their choosing during launches. The tech team also has a watercooler channel for posting random news, interesting articles, pointless debates, and GIFs to mimic the camaraderie and inanity that happens over coffee in the kitchen when everyone works together.

FASTER DOESN'T MEAN YOU'RE DONE IN A WEEK

The methods we've introduced in this chapter can be adopted by any manager and take little time and no or little money. To drive home the value of devoting serious consideration to this, we close by describing the most impressive example of getting people up to speed we've ever encountered, which not coincidentally is conducted by one of the most successful companies you may have never heard of: the Danaher Corporation. The story here also highlights a last key practice that all managers should consider adopting: Continue onboarding new team members for at least the first three months.

We've mentioned Danaher a few times in this book, but you might not know much about them. Danaher makes essential stuff for science and technology professionals, from high-tech microscopes, to medical diagnostic devices, to water testing equipment. That may not sound sexy, but since the late 1960s, only Berkshire Hathaway and Altria have outpaced Danaher in return to shareholders; Microsoft and Oracle have done so since their 1986 initial public offerings, but that's about it. So, the lesser known Danaher is in rarified company, and the company's story is pertinent to our discussion because people here are organized into fluid teams and there is a steady ebb-and-flow of personnel among locations. And they are always hiring new associates (Danaher's term for everyone who works there, from employees to managers to executives).

We got to know this terrific company a few years ago when CEO Tom Joyce asked us to kick off an associate engagement initiative with a speech to his senior leaders. We quickly discovered that Danaher's ambitious, hard-charging people have almost unbounded career opportunities to move between teams and learn and grow. CEO Joyce himself started out as a marketing project manager in Danaher's tools group in 1989. But it's also a culture that takes some getting used to. Which is why, says Angie Lalor, senior vice president of human resources, the company sees its onboarding process as vital to its success. But the process wasn't always so effective.

Lalor said, "On too many occasions we were bringing very successful people into the company and they were struggling, in some cases they failed. It was a failure on how we were bringing them on board. They didn't have a good enough understanding of the culture and the Danaher Business System (DBS)—how important DBS is to their jobs and how we lead our teams."

To understand Danaher, one must understand DBS, the company's unique continuous improvement process that drives every aspect of the organization, from lean manufacturing to innovation and leadership. It pushes every associate to stretch for never-ending improvements. Unlike similar methodologies in some businesses—which might be housed in the manufacturing department alone—DBS is the soul of every Danaher team. And does it ever work. The company has an amazing record of acquiring companies, then improving their operations and driving substantial performance and growth. Danaher has provided around 20 percent annual returns to shareholders for more than two decades.

Danaher's process for bringing new hires onboard is called Immersion, is customized for each person and function specific (which means it's different for general managers, operations leaders, sales professionals, scientists, or engineers, etc.), and is especially designed to help people understand the importance of DBS and their role in championing a DBS culture.

Which means that, for up to three months after joining the company, a new associate will not go to her specific operating company and will not assume any of her regular duties. She won't answer email, take phone calls, or go to regular team meetings. It doesn't matter if she is going to be the president of an operating company or work a few layers down, she'll spend those months learning. The time is spent benchmarking, visiting other operating companies, job shadowing, and developing a network that will help in the future. The new associate will also visit customers, learn about Danaher technologies, and, most importantly, see DBS in action.

As such, the new hire will be part of at least a couple of weeklong "kaizen" process improvement events. "These are long days, often from six o'clock in the morning until nine at night problemsolving," said Lalor. "New leaders will work side by side with experienced machine operators and the most junior operator in a cell to improve a process. It's an incredibly rich way to learn and understand culturally the stretch-approach to continuous improvement."

And during the entire process, the new hire will keep a detailed *Immersion Journal* about what she learns, and then takes about an hour every week to review the learnings with her supervisor and sometimes another mentor.

Antoine Preisig went through a three-month-long Immersion process before assuming his role as general manager for the Europe, Middle East, and Africa Region of X-Rite, one of Danaher's operating companies. He told us, "I have to admit I came in to Immersion apprehensive. I'd been working for twenty-five years in good companies (Dell and Logitech). I had good business skills. I wondered, am I going to get reprogrammed? As I was going through the sessions, my defenses started to lessen. I realized this is the culture I want to work with."

Immersion is shorter for individual contributors, but still involves action-based learning that helps every new associate understand the context of where they fit and build a network of associates to call upon.

Now, while we'd love to see all teams adopt a formal method as rigorous as Danaher's for getting people up to speed, we know that's just not on the radar for most of us. However, all team leaders can go a long way to achieving comparable results by customizing onboarding plans for each new hire, and by extending the process past the initial honeymoon period for at least ninety days.

A few basic ideas for the three-month process for bringing new people up to speed include:

✓ Assign a mentor (or several) so the new person can job shadow and learn more about the team and organization.
✓ Ensure early projects and goals are challenging yet eminently achievable.

✓ Meet at least monthly on each employee's career development in an aspirational conversation.

✓ Invite and encourage social interactions with team members and those outside the team.

✓ Meet several times over the first month to provide context about the team and the organization and answer any questions about the big picture.

✓ Meet at least weekly in one-on-ones about performance goals and assignments.

✓ Assign a stretch project tied to the corporate goals that will help the person get outside the team, meet people around the organization, and better understand the value their team brings to the entire organization.

FOUR

CHALLENGE EVERYTHING

Inspire Innovation Through Healthy Discord

A survey of Bell Helicopter's customers showed the company's copters were seen as reliable and safe, but not particularly innovative. If people knew the Bell name, they often associated it with the Hueys of the Vietnam War. New CEO Mitch Snyder wanted to break the eighty-year-old company out of its routine and habits, so within weeks of taking over as the company's senior leader in 2015 he brought together an Innovation Team composed of engineers and paired them with graphic artists and creative designers, many of whom had worked in the video game or movie industry. The artists had backgrounds in creating out-of-this-world spaceships and military transports for digital storytelling, sci-fi movies, and video games, but had little idea about the technical requirements of flight. The engineers were used to creating helicopters that were safe and efficient but not particularly imaginative.

"It sounds like a simple idea, but it was anything but," recalls

Snyder. "We put the two teams together, and there was a lot of skepticism."

Robert Hastings, the company's chief of staff, sat in on some of the Innovation Team's early meetings. He told us: "The designers would say, 'What if the wings looked like this.' And the engineers would say, 'Nope.' So the designers would try again, 'How about if the wings looked like this?' Engineers: 'Nope. Won't fly.' It was like watching ping pong."

Innovation team leader Scott Drennan recalls teasing the designers that they "were giving us the Buck Rodgers or *Battlestar Galactica* treatment."

But Snyder wasn't about to give up. "We moved them all together in one room, full time." And he set some ground rules. "We created a safe area. I know it's basic, but we made the debate open. We said there were no stupid ideas; you can throw anything out." The team was told that they were expected to respond to all ideas, no matter how seemingly crazy or uninformed, respectfully. "The rule was: No one laughs or criticizes, and you must find a way to accept at least part of any idea," he said.

Team meetings were fierce. The CEO recalls, "I would go into some of their working rooms and they'd say, 'We think it's better if you leave.' Tensions were that high. But I'd go by one of our restaurants later that afternoon and they were all in there having lunch together. Fire in the trenches makes people tighter."

Said engineer Drennan, "I knew it was working when all those 'That'll never works' turned into this quiet little whisper in the corner that said, 'You know, that might work.'"

The revolutionary ideas that emerged from this team will serve as "a roadmap for the future of rotary flight," according to an article in one industry publication. Snyder is more than a little proud of that reviewer's headline: "What if Lamborghini and Tesla designed a helicopter."

In addition, the openness and collaboration have allowed team members to learn an extraordinary amount from one another. The CEO said, "The designers have learned more about aerodynamics and the mechanics of how aircraft fly as well as safety aspects, and our engineers got to understand design and the way people relate to creativity and imagery better. In one of our meetings recently, someone said, 'Why don't we put this line here?' and one of the creative designers said, 'No, that won't work aerodynamically.' You don't know who are the designers and who are the engineers anymore. They've become a real collaborative team. They are now so engaged, so proud of themselves and each other. It's not one group sitting on one side or the other anymore, they are united."

Snyder has fostered instinctively what Harvard Business School Professor Amy Edmonson calls psychological safety. Recall that at Google, the Project Aristotle researchers found the degree of psychological safety team members felt was *the* most important factor in driving high performance in that company. So, what exactly is it? Edmonson defines psychological safety as, "A climate in which the focus can be on productive discussion that enables early prevention of problems and the accomplishment of shared goals because people are less likely to focus on self-protection."

At Bell Helicopter, said engineer Drennan, it's psychological safety that is driving the innovation engine, "giving us permission to fail, to drive beyond historical rules and process, to disrupt our business model and radically innovate. We are more like a pack now hunting for solutions rather than a herd searching for cover."

The research backs up this idea. It shows team performance is enhanced when all members feel comfortable speaking out about problems—even about mistakes they've made—and can feel free to ask questions, seek honest feedback, disagree with colleagues, challenge assumptions, and share ideas—even ones that fly in the face of the prevailing sentiment on the team. Also, in high-performance environments, team members have confidence that coworkers, and their manager, will not penalize them or think less of them if they ask for help.

Lance Trenary, CEO of restaurant chain Golden Corral, has a simple rule in his firm, "Never shoot the messenger." When a team member says something completely opposite to prevailing wisdom, he said it's vital that others allow the idea to be heard and debated. "We also try to make sure people get a lot of credit for a great idea, so they realize we celebrate new ways of thinking."

Yet, in extensive studies of work teams across a wide range of industries, Edmonson found employees often feel a degree of risk if they speak up on their teams. Many of us worry we'll be seen as ignorant or annoying if we ask too many questions, incompetent if we admit our missteps, or disruptive or insubordinate if we challenge prevailing thinking. We fear embarrassment if we offer up ideas that are unconventional. (But what innovation isn't?) And it's not just the skittish among us, but often bold teammates are concerned as well.

Let's put this into a few real scenarios: Imagine a nurse reads a patient's chart and is fairly sure the dosage of a medicine is wrong, but she goes ahead and administers the drug because the doctor in charge has told her before not to challenge his orders. Or suppose a first officer is copiloting a passenger jet with his captain and believes the senior officer is making a serious error in judgment on the approach for landing, but doesn't speak up because he's not as experienced. Or picture a recently hired vice president sitting in her first executive team meeting, listening to her new colleagues talk optimistically about a pending merger. She is familiar with the company in question and has serious reservations, but she's the newbie and doesn't want to appear negative.

We've found in today's highest-performing team environments, members feel extremely comfortable offering one another proactive feedback, speaking up even when their advice hasn't been asked for. Indeed, one sure sign of a healthy team is that employees offer each other tough-to-hear feedback, instead of offloading all problems to the boss and hoping they trickle down. Does that ever happen?

There are definite business benefits to this approach to team leadership. Employees on the front lines have valuable insights about how the organization can be improved. Ricardo Semler, CEO of Semco in Brazil, has a core value in his company of "democracy," which means lots of employee involvement. "Clearly, workers who control their working conditions are going to be happier than workers who don't," he said. "But about 90 percent of the time, participatory management is just hot air."

Semler's commitment to the concept was put to the test when his company needed to build a bigger plant for its marine division. "Real estate agents looked for months and found nothing. So we asked the employees to help, and over the first weekend they found three factories for sale, all of them nearby. We closed up shop for a day, piled everyone into buses, and drove out to inspect the buildings. Then the workers voted—and they chose a plant the counselors didn't really want. It was an interesting situation—one that tested our commitment to participatory management," he said.

Semler and the leadership team accepted the employees' decision because, "letting people participate in the decisions that affect their lives will have a positive effect on employee motivation and morale." The company bought the building and moved in, and workers designed a layout for a flexible manufacturing system. "That plant really belongs to its employees. I feel like a guest every time I walk in," said the CEO.

The results: The division's productivity—as measured by dollars earned per employee—jumped three-fold, and market share of marine sales grew from 54 to 62 percent.

It's baffling that so many managers still resist listening to their people regarding decisions that affect their work, let alone inviting such input as Semler did. Not that managers' intentions are bad, it's just that getting employees involved can be messy and time consuming—it's much easier to talk about it than do it.

But to drive real innovation, we've found the best teams participate collaboratively in a freewheeling sharing of ideas. The popular notion of a lone maverick coming up with a cure for cancer or inventing the iPod is a romantic myth. The best leaders we speak with credit their success to avid idea-sharing within and between teams—not to a handful of geniuses.

IT STARTS WITH THE MANAGER

Now, it may seem that safe debate and openness would naturally thrive more in innovative corporate cultures—for instance, wouldn't a team at Apple necessarily be more conducive to this type of thing than a team in an old-line manufacturing company or a small business focused on car repair? Or perhaps it could be argued that the kind of work your team is tasked with will make a big difference—if you are in research and development wouldn't avid debate and open sharing of ideas make more sense? What about teams that are primarily tasked with executing on procedures? Would the manager of a warehouse, call center, restaurant, emergency room, insurance agency, or other such process-oriented team really want employees making recommendations for improvements all the time? Or, what about teams that are pressed for *time*—do leaders of these teams have enough hours in the day to engage in open debates? Or, what about the potential *disruption* of debating—wouldn't arguments among team members cause distractions in open environment offices? Finally, what about the *rules*—what if a company has strict performance measurement processes that require managers to keep tabs on employee errors and report them?

Certainly, every team leader must work within constraints regarding how much debate and idea-generation can be encouraged. And yes, leaders must keep their people focused to assure that goals are achieved and customers served in a timely manner. Fair enough. Of course, there is a time and place for openness and discussion, and there are occasions when you have to follow policy and get a job done. But every manager can do more to foster psychological safety among their team members, and every team can use more creativity and drive. It's amazing, as we conduct workshops within organizations, how often senior leaders of seemingly process-driven environments ask us to push their people to take more smart risks and challenge the status quo. They are desperate for ingenuity.

Professor Edmonson stresses that strict performance goals are in no way anathema to developing greater psychological safety within a team. Quite the contrary, clarity of goals and personal and team accountability help motivate members. "Psychological safety . . . can enhance the motivating effects of goals," she added, and does not mean that team members feel "an absence of pressure."

So, how can managers best foster this kind of culture—where people feel safe to speak up and have their voices heard, but still feel positive pressure to achieve?

Ray Dalio, founder of Bridgewater Associates (the world's largest hedge fund), says it must start with radical transparency. He illustrates how this works by sharing a scathing email he received from one of his employees (Jim Haskel) after a meeting. "Ray, you deserve a D- for your performance today in the meeting," wrote the employee. "You did not prepare at all because there is no way you could have and been that disorganized. In the future, I/we would ask you to take some time and prepare . . . we can't let this happen again."

Instead of being irritated, Dalio circulated the email to all Bridgewater employees. "I need feedback like that," he said.

Dalio says such honesty makes for a more meritocratic work environment where the best ideas emerge and debate can flourish. But, he says, there are a few exceptions: "You don't have to tell people that their bald spot is growing or their baby is ugly," he said with a smile.

Below are a core set of the most effective practices for team leaders we've seen in action to practice transparency like that and enhance feelings of psychological safety in modern work groups:

- Decrease the power distance between you and your team.
- Set rules for debate, and take a turn leading it.
- Diligently and publicly ask questions of team members, at all levels.
- Listen to your radicals.
- Create latitude for risk-taking and failure.
- Set strict team goals and monitor them transparently.

We'll address each of these ideas.

HIERARCHY DOESN'T MEAN YOU ARE ALWAYS RIGHT

Of course, few of today's leaders are the autocratic and inaccessible jerks sometimes portrayed in popular media (Mr. Burns comes to mind). But we've surveyed more than 850,000 employees over the past few years, and these people make it remarkably clear that many modern managers still give off the vibe: "I just don't have time for your input or questions." Most often because of their harried schedules, or perhaps they don't see the need, too many managers put the kibosh on employees' willingness to challenge the status quo and speak up. We had the unhappy experience of being part of a team led by such a manager. When a company we worked for years ago decided to create a cross-functional team to increase professional services revenue, we thought it was a great idea. We went in to the experience with the highest of expectations, and we began in the first meeting to attempt to initiate open discussion and debate—with the executive in charge and others. We were confused as to why none of our peers was participating, but it became clear after the meeting. The executive in charge stormed into our offices, shut the door, and let us know, in no uncertain terms, "You will never again contradict me in front of my employees."

We did, but still.

Outbursts like that leave everyone confused. After all, isn't hashing out different views the point of bringing cross-functional teams together? Contrast that attitude to what Apple founder Steve Jobs said about debates in his team meetings. When asked if his team members were willing to tell him if they thought he was wrong, Jobs laughed. "Oh yeah, we have wonderful arguments," he said. When asked if he won those arguments, he was adamant, "Oh no, you can't. If you want to hire great people and have them stay working for you, you have to let them make a lot of decisions and be run by the best ideas, not hierarchy. The best ideas have to win."

Now, by accounts from those closest to him, Jobs hardly lacked for a strong point of view, and he argued his positions with great force. He was also a tough task master. And that's why he was such a terrific role model for this practice. He held the highest of standards for input and accountability, but he was willing to listen and be swayed. He wanted debate. He demanded it. He knew it would make his team and the company's products better.

Now, in an effort to undercut the tendency of the hierarchical management structure to make employees feel like minions, cogs in a management machine, for the past few years some companies have tried flattening their organizational charts. It seems fairly logical. After all, in too many workplaces, employees tell us they feel as if they are supposed to keep their opinions to themselves and let the bosses make the decisions, so wouldn't flattening help employees at all levels feel more ownership of challenges and successes. In theory, flattening would also speed-up decisions by diffusing responsibility, and make companies more inventive and nimble by being more responsive to customer demands and to problems arising on the frontlines.

Unfortunately, getting rid of hierarchy hasn't worked that well. Modern teams need the accountability a manager provides as much as ever, as well as the direction and guidance. What we have seen help, however, is a reduction in power distance.

To understand that concept, we turn to the work of sociologist Geert Hofstede, who has quantified power distance in more than one hundred countries. A high power-distance means that a boss is typically the undisputed ruler of his team—his word is law— while in countries with lower scores, employees typically feel more safe to take initiative and challenge the status quo. Managers in low power-distance environments give their employees a lot more rein, getting involved primarily when there are challenges to overcome or successes to celebrate. Hofstede says Chinese workplaces have a high average power distance of eighty, Japanese teams about fifty-four, workplaces in the United States average about forty, United Kingdom cultures around thirty-five, while Danish teams—with a score of eighteen—have one of the lowest average power distances in the world (only Israel and Austria score lower).

In Denmark, managing isn't seen as particularly prestigious like it is in other parts of the world. Being a manager is just another role on the team to be accomplished. And a widely acknowledged part of a manager's job is to create feelings of openness and affiliation with teammates by involving them respectfully in solving problems, sincerely recognizing their unique accomplishments, and ensuring all voices are heard.

The Danes actually have a word for all this collegiality, it's *arbejdsglæde*. While it may look like something created by accidentally sitting on a computer keyboard, it is a euphonic mixture of two roots: *Arbejde*, which means work, and *glæde*, or happiness. So *arbejdsglæde* is "happiness at work" or "work joy" (pronouncing it "ah-bides-glude" is fairly close). And there's a payoff. Considering only five million people live here, Denmark has produced a surprising number of innovations including magnetic storage, the loudspeaker, dry-cell batteries, insulin, the fiberscope, and the Lego brick to name just a few. The country is also number one in the entire world for the percentage of happy people, number six in GDP per capita (the United States is tenth), and number four with the highest percentage of satisfied and loyal employees (behind only Belgium, Norway, and Costa Rica). And while Gallup has found that 18 percent of U.S. workers are actively disengaged—meaning they are emotionally disconnected from the vision and values of their workplaces—that number is only half as high in Danish teams.

Interesting that we can learn about a soft skill like psychological safety from a land built by Vikings (known more for pillaging than touchy-feely stuff).

Workplace equality in Denmark is even regulated. Any company with more than thirty-five employees is required to open at least one seat on its board for an employee representative, elected by their peers. This board member serves for a time before giving the opportunity to another employee. The employees who serve do so on an equal footing and have the same voting powers as all other board members.

The point of all of this: The less dominating power exerted by a manager, the more inclusiveness she creates, and the more groups are willing to participate and generate ideas.

Team managers don't need a corporate initiative to create this kind of inclusiveness. They can simply employ practices at the team level that inspire their people to speak up and be bolder in sharing ideas and engaging in more avid debate. One of these is to actually schedule debates and lead them—following a core set of respectful ground rules. That's next.

HARMONY IS OVERRATED

The most effective and innovative teams we've studied have regular, intense debates—which has been fun for us to observe. The ability to disagree, without causing offense, is essential to robust communication and problem-solving within teams. Yet when we pose the question to groups of leaders what's better—a team that's almost always harmonious or one that has conflicts and arguments—the vast majority vote for a team with no disharmony. The irony is that teammates *want* the opportunity to challenge each other. As long as discussions are respectful and everyone gets the chance to contribute equally, most people thrive on this kind of debate—finding it not only intellectually stimulating but important to getting to the route of problems and working out optimal solutions. Teams feel more bonded and more effective when they regularly engage in challenging discussions, when members are encouraged to argue with one another's ideas and perspectives. It's also true even if the debates get a little heated.

Still, anyone who has ever been in an argument at work knows how hard it can be for people to keep their cool. You may even have had someone become resentful with you and try to retaliate after a disagreement. That's why managers have to set ground rules for healthy debate, and they need to actively run many of these discussions, at least at first—modeling the right behaviors: How to make a point, ask questions of colleagues deferentially, and not take themselves too seriously. It's also the job of team leaders to ensure that all members understand discussions are not to be hijacked by one or two strong voices, but that everyone must be given a chance to speak up.

Just about every team leader we interviewed had explicitly established ground rules for debate within their teams. We recommend considering these:

- Treat each other with respect (challenge the position not the person, and don't make it personal).
- Listen to one another carefully before responding, and ask for clarification if needed (seek to gather facts; and do not jump to conclusions).
- Come to the debate ready to present facts and data (not supposition)
- Remember you are *not* in a competition to win (debates are opportunities to find the best ideas, be enlightened, and learn—not score points or ram home your points).
- After the team makes a decision collaboratively, we

are going to support it (even if it wasn't our idea or we might have reservations).

One manager who actively monitors and steers these kinds of debates in his team is Mark Beck, CEO of JELD-WEN, a global window and door manufacturer with 20,000 employees. He told us that it's up to leaders to step in and protect their people when things get heated. "Sometimes you use simple levity," he said. "Our CFO is really good at this. At particularly tense moments, he says in a loud parental voice, 'Now everybody just settle down,' and then he cracks a smile and everyone laughs. It instantly takes the tension down a notch or two."

In some cases, Beck says, he might take the side of a person whose view is under assault, even if he doesn't necessarily agree with it. This isn't gamesmanship, it's to show that the person is offering up a reasonable way of thinking that should be respected. "The attacker usually steps back a little and softens their tone when a leader does that," he said.

And, Beck adds, managers must take the lead in getting everyone participating by posing the right questions. Below are just a few examples of some great questions we've heard team leaders throw out in debates:

- That's a good thought, walk us through the process you went through to reach that conclusion?
- What rules should we be breaking here?
- What's our biggest risk in this, and what's our fallback position?

- What if we did nothing at all, what would happen?
- Are we missing anything?
- What do we have to do to come up with a solution together?
- Aside from earning us a profit, how would this decision change lives and make the world a better place?

Beck said that smart questions can encourage active debate when a team has plateaued or is stuck in a safe zone. At times of such inertia, he'll tell his direct reports, "The only way you can get your topic on the management team agenda is to frame it out as a question; and collectively we have to come up with an answer."

This CEO also made a great point about how "changing the question"—or formulating the question at play in a new way—can recharge problem-solving. Beck told us the instructive story of a team he managed when he was with a previous employer. At the time, he was assigned to turn around one of that company's heavy-duty manufacturing businesses. "The business was in crisis, and customer orders were languishing," he said. "The question the team had been asking was 'How do we survive?' We realized that was the wrong question. We turned it into, 'How can we come out of this crisis in an improved position?'"

That emboldened the team. They concluded the only way to make the business profitable, and to deliver the quality and quantity of products customers needed, was to make additional investments in process improvement and capacity. To that end, they would have to substantially change the business model. But the company's leadership and board of directors would not approve hundreds of millions of dollars of investment in a same-old approach. "We felt that a new business model with a bold and aggressive set of actions was our only hope," he said.

And bold it was. The team's plan comprised: streamlining the customer base and product offering; improving manufacturing efficiency with new technologies and methodologies that would change the way products were made; raising prices to cover costs; and, ensuring viability and stability by signing long-term, binding agreements with their customers. Beck outlined it this way, "Essentially we were offering a select few customers a greater level of long-term supply assurance if they would agree to a new way of doing business together."

Was it popular with those customers? Hardly. Every single one fought the move, but eventually through careful negotiation, all began to see this was the only viable way forward for everyone. The business started to become profitable, and more important, began to have the capacity to deliver enough products to help its customers grow.

That meant the team was soon in a position to build a new factory to meet demand. Thus ensued another debate, with some on the team arguing to build the facility in the United States, others wanting to put it in China. The anticipated ROI was within the margin of error for each location, so Beck asked his board members. They were split too. The math didn't take the team anywhere, those above were divided, so what was the right decision?

Said Beck, "We again changed the question. We turned it from 'Where can we make the most money?' to, 'In which location will we be able to earn an acceptable return, given the Black Swans we may face?'" In referring to Black Swans, Beck is using the term popularized by Nassim Nicholas Taleb, professor at New

York University, in his book *The Black Swan*, to describe major events that defy expectations and carry a punishing wallop.

Beck and the team brainstormed ten potential Black Swan scenarios that might occur in the near term, such as China deciding to let its currency float and the U.S. electing a new president who starts a trade war. The team assigned a probability of likeliness to each Black Swan.

Next, under each Black Swan, the team determined the potential return that would be earned by a factory in the United States and one in China. "In about 90 percent of cases we could make an acceptable return in the U.S., but in only 50 percent we could make an acceptable return in China," he said. "I didn't make the decision; it was unanimous by the time the team went through this debate." And so today, that company has a nice new plant in New York state.

One last example of changing the question. When Beck arrived at JELD-WEN, the company's focus was on getting ready to issue an initial public offering (selling its stock to the public for the first time). He changed the question to: "How do we get ready to become a Fortune 500 company?" Yes, JELD-WEN did issue an IPO, and it was wildly successful (fifteen-times oversubscribed and shares rose 30 percent in the first month), "But that's been because we were focused on building a Fortune 500 company," he said. "If we had just focused on the IPO and seen that as the finish line, I don't think our story would have resonated with investors in the same way."

Because his teams stick to respectful ground rules, Beck estimates they are able to come to consensus about 99 percent of the time. "If it's done right, there's usually no need for a leader to have to make a decision, it's become obvious to everyone. I might just say, 'Let me summarize what I think we are all saying.'"

But, of course, even in the healthiest of teams, there are times when one person or a small collective digs in—wanting to zag right when everyone else has already made a mental zig to the left. When all the arguments have been made, Beck says, "If the horse has all four legs pointing up, the leader has to state the obvious. But you can still do it in a way that doesn't seem like someone's won and someone's lost. A leader might say, 'The arguments on both sides have been fantastic. I can see why reasonable people could go either way. But we've got to make a decision. Here's why I think we need to go this way.' Then, the next time, people on the team won't be afraid to make a stand. No one will feel like they've lost; each teammate will know the leader appreciates his or her honest input."

DILIGENTLY AND PUBLICLY SEEK DIVERSE OPINIONS

Effective leaders like Beck are genuinely curious to learn the views and ideas of employees. They ask lots of questions of people in meetings and get conversations rolling, and that encourages everyone to truly engage. They also seek input from every voice, especially from lower-status team members who otherwise might be reluctant to speak up.

We were told a great story of this by Linda Kaplan Thaler, who then was serving as chairman of New York City ad agency Publicis Kaplan Thaler. When her company was tasked with creating a promotion on breast cancer awareness for the Lifetime network, the firm assembled its best creative minds. A young intern sat in the shadows. It was one of her first brainstorming sessions, and she was not about to speak up among the creative geniuses who had developed wildly successful ad campaigns like the Aflac Duck and "I don't want to grow up, I'm a Toys 'R' us kid." But Kaplan Thaler pled and cajoled the young intern into sharing something . . . anything. The chairman told us: "The intern said, 'This may be totally crazy, but when my friends and I sign off on our messages to each other, we always end it with *You're my bra*. It means you're my support, my lift. It's probably too crazy, I can't believe I just said that.'"

That crazy idea turned into Lifetimes' national breast cancer awareness campaign starring Whoopie Goldberg. "It became this huge thing," said Kaplan Thaler. "Why? Because we said don't be inhibited. Share any crazy idea. Think if this young woman had never been invited to a meeting or never raised her hand, or hadn't felt comfortable in sharing. We wouldn't have had a campaign that was so memorable."

To pull out the best ideas, team leaders should pay close attention to whether all members agree with the direction of a team discussion, or if one or two haven't weighed in. Beck told us, "If the group is starting to form consensus but one person doesn't agree, you can usually see it in their face. I might say, 'It looks like you aren't quite buying this. What do you think?' If they don't speak up, you have to ask them to."

Jose Maria Zas, leader of the Latin America market for American Express Global Card Services, says he pushes his team to come to debates not with complaints but with alternative solutions—from the crazy to the conservative. And he encourages everyone to voice their opinions. "I remember a time when I led a team in a highly vocal culture where people used to speak over each other. I introduced the use of a stone. I told everyone they will each have their opportunity to speak; however, by turn, and the person speaking will be the one with the stone in their hands. Simple, yes. But it was effective."

Managers too often allow a handful of powerful voices to dominate and too quickly shut off discussion and questioning. We understand the need to move on. Let's face it, questions can be annoying and time is always limited. But it's important for leaders to fight the impulse to dissuade inquiries. Adrian will always remember a high school classmate who modeled terrific behavior. While most of the students in his twelfth-grade math class suffered through lectures with a stoic cluelessness, keeping as quiet as mice to avoid admitting their ignorance, one bright student named Emily would not hesitate to raise her hand and say, "I don't get it." The teacher would then explain a particularly dense concept again, at which Emily would either nod, and the teacher would move on, or she'd shake her head and say, "Nope, still don't get it. Am I the only one?" She would literally *demand* clarity. She was fearless. And Adrian's entire class learned a whole lot more because of it.

CAPITALIZE ON THE WISDOM OF RADICALS

Of course, some team members don't need much encouragement to share their views. Many of the great teams we've studied have at least one member who could be described as a *radical*. Richard Hackman called them *deviants*. Hackman was a professor of social and organizational psychology at Yale and then

Harvard and was perhaps the preeminent thinker on teamwork of his time. He said, "Every team needs a deviant, someone who can help the team by challenging the tendency to want too much homogeneity, which can stifle creativity and learning. (They) are the ones who stand back and say, 'Wait a minute, why are we even doing this at all? What if we looked at the thing backwards or turned it inside out?' That's when people say, 'Oh, no, no, no, that's ridiculous,' and so the discussion about what's ridiculous comes up."

In many workplaces, however, managers tell their radicals—in no uncertain terms—to keep their radicalness to themselves. Great leaders leverage their contrariness.

Hackman said, "In our research, we looked carefully at teams that produced something original and those that were merely average, where nothing really sparkled. It turned out that the teams with deviants outperformed teams without them. In many cases, deviant thinking is a source of great innovation."

As you might imagine, people who veer from the norm often do so at great personal cost. Our high school chum Emily probably knew she might be ostracized from her schoolmates—most of whom, Adrian included, worried only about getting through a day without some humiliation befalling them. Yet radicals are willing to say the thing that nobody else is. And that means they can raise people's level of anxiety—especially that of their leaders.

"When the boat is floating with the current, it really is extraordinarily courageous for somebody to stand up and say, 'We've got to pause and probably change direction,'" said Hackman. On most teams, no one wants to hear that, which is precisely why many team leaders crack down on radicals and try to get them to stop asking difficult questions and making off-the-wall suggestions. Maybe they even bump them off the team.

In Hackman's research, however, he found that when a team loses its radical voice it often becomes mediocre.

When we speak about this concept of radicals to some groups, often a few folks will come up after and let us know that it struck a chord. The first thing we ask is if they are truly radicals, or devil's advocates. Because the two are very different.

One CEO told us devil's advocates are "cheap intellectuals," scoring points by taking potshots at any new idea. A radical doesn't offer up only negativity for negativity's sake, he's arguing to look at things from a different perspective—especially the customer's—and more importantly is known for offering up fresh, even wacky ideas. People used to say of Winston Churchill that he'd have ten ideas a day, one of which wasn't half bad.

A devil's advocate, however, looks only at the negative.

Tom Kelley, general manager of IDEO, the world-famous design firm, said, "The devil's advocate may be the biggest innovation killer in America today." These people see only downsides, problems, disasters-in-waiting. "Once those floodgates open, they can drown a new initiative in negativity," he said.

Instead, Kelley's work shows that people who are radical in their thinking push the work of innovation forward by assuming various *positive* personas. They may take the form of "anthropologists," who bring new insights to the team by observing human nature—especially that of end users; "experimenters" who prototype new ideas continuously; or "cross-pollinators" who explore other teams or industries and bring back learnings and fit them into the needs of their teams.

When Scott O'Neil took over as senior vice president of team marketing and business operations for the National Basketball Association, he told us that team meetings were devoid of constructive debate. One of his team members, Chris Heck, recalled, "We all thought Scott wanted to hear that he was doing a great job. But he took me aside after one of the first staff meetings and asked me to start disagreeing with him—about anything. He wanted to open discussions up to conflict, to show that it was a safe environment in which to disagree. It was a great concept and it really worked." There's a leader who realized he might have to plant his first radical, which also works.

THERE'S NO SUCCESS WITHOUT SOME FAILURE

There's been much hoopla in recent years about failure, out of Silicon Valley especially. Mantras have arisen about failing, sometimes too blithely suggesting that all failure is good if it teaches us a lesson. Tell that to a patient about to undergo heart surgery. No, what great teams teach their members is how to fail in *smart* ways, and to accept that some failure is inevitable in teams pushing to innovate and improve. In fact, if teams aren't experiencing some smart failures along the way, they're probably not being creative enough or taking enough risks.

One of the hallmarks of the highest performing teams is that they feel relatively comfortable taking a chance. This doesn't mean members are not held accountable for being judicious, but managers have created latitude when their people are being bold. The key is that risks should be focused on making a customer experience better, and yes the team must rigorously learn from them.

Now, of course, failure doesn't always result from taking a risk. Sometimes mistakes are due to a lack of understanding or skill. Managers must send the message that these types of failures will happen too, and the important thing is to be honest and fess up so that they can be corrected quickly. One way team leaders can inspire comfort in the admission of mistakes by team members is to acknowledge their own fallibility. Saying things to your team like, "I'm likely to miss things or mess up now and then, so I need to hear from you when I do," gives employees the assurance that no one is going to be held to unrealistic standards of perfection.

When he was CEO of Canadian Tire, the 58,000 person retailer, Wayne Sales told us an example of public admission and vulnerability that struck a chord with him early in his career. Chrysler had let executives drive new vehicles, but with the odometers disconnected. "When this was discovered, I can only imagine what was happening within the organization," said Sales. "The legal counsel was most likely advising, 'You must deny this, you must spin this.' In doing the right thing, Lee Iacocca (then Chrysler CEO) said, 'We made a mistake. We breached the trust and integrity of our customers. We acknowledge we did this, and we promise it will never happen again.' And you know what? Life went on."

Imagine if Iacocca had put a marketing spin on the situation, had denied wrongdoing but been later proven wrong. We might still be talking about it in ethics classes. Instead, he admitted fault—even though he likely had nothing to do with the mistake—and his reputation, and the company's, actually benefited from the admission.

In a similar vein, managers need to explicitly encourage their people to come to them about mistakes made and problems as they are developing, and in a timely fashion so the best job of damage-control can be done. Our favorite example to inspire such open-ness is from sales guru Jeffrey Gitomer. He told us that not long ago he began handing out cash bonuses to his employees when they admitted a mistake. "The results were astounding," he said. "I found that people were so surprised and emotionally relieved that many times they actually cried when I gave them the reward. I realized that people didn't make mistakes on purpose, and many times the mistakes were in an effort to succeed, or simply trying to navigate uncharted waters." It's gotten so that now one of his employees, fresh from a major mess-up, will sheepishly enter his office and say, "I think I need a bonus."

Returning to the point of risk-taking to spur more creative idea generation, here managers must give license to their teams to experiment. Dictums such as "fail fast" are wise in that they assume the team will correct its mistakes quickly and that failures are incremental in nature—leading to a better outcome. As any scientist will tell you, the process of discovery hardly ever follows the formula of hypothesis, test, and eureka. It almost always comes through an untidy process of trial, error, and improvement that unfolds over time.

When Bell Helicopter CEO Mitch Snyder kick-started the innovation of more creative helicopter designs in his firm, he had his team implement new processes of rapid prototyping and test-ing. While engineers in the past had done all they could to avoid failures during development, which is a logical mandate for any end product that goes up in the air, their safe approach meant that new product development typically took years and years as team members methodically thought through every contingency.

He told us at one point his engineers were stuck toying with an elaborate eight-foot prototype of a new VTOL (vertical take-off and landing) aircraft, but still hadn't subjected it to flight tests outside. Snyder gave the team the latitude to aggressively test, to spend the company's money even if it meant crashes of the unmanned craft. After a few days the engineers came back with a response: They would build a yet smaller sub-scale model that could be tested in a wind tunnel. That, to be blunt, was not at all what Snyder was looking for. He sent them back to the drawing board and pushed them to put the larger sub-scale aircraft in the air, and fast.

He says that now, the team has adopted the motto Fail Fast, Fix Fast, and Forget Fast, and they've become comfortable with incremental failures. "The other day they brought in a video of one of their big babies that were super excited about," he recounted of one large, unmanned prototype. "They showed me the video of it crashing. They worked on it over the weekend, and got it up and flying again."

Now, not every team can learn through prototyping, but it's still possible for everyone to make room for intelligent failures in the process of improving. The first step is defining what smart failures looks like—specifically—in your team. We all understand what success looks like on our teams, but wouldn't it be helpful to know the right and wrong ways to fail? Perhaps a smart failure might be one made in the pursuit of a goal that was ambitious, audacious even. Or perhaps it might be a thoughtful and well-researched project that for some reason just didn't work—the technology wasn't ready or customers didn't accept it.

Leaders also need to model the behavior of failing. If a leader preaches risk-taking but never fails himself, or never admits it, then consequently the team will take few gambles themselves.

Finally, it's important to publicly reward people who take a risk and fail—just as much as you do successes. Indian conglomerate Tata has a program in which they award the year's best attempts with the Dare to Try Award. It is presented to the most thoughtful and well-executed failures. When the company first launched the program in 2008, few teams entered. But when everyone saw the winners get congratulated on stage by the CEO, within three years 132 teams had submitted for the prize.

TRACK TEAM GOALS TRANSPARENTLY

The final part we have found in challenging everything is to establish clear team goals and chart progress toward them openly. It might seem this could make team members feel threatened, as though their feet are being held to the fire; but, in reality, transparency of this sort encourages people to feel they are working, in the inimitable words of Alexandre Dumas's Musketeers, all for one and one for all. It actually takes pressure off individuals to work toward team goals collectively, especially if the goals are simple to understand, realistic, and the metrics for tracking them are well-devised.

Edmonson of Harvard highlights the positive results of such transparency of goals, going so far as to assert: "The act of goal-setting can be as or more important than the goal itself, because it creates shared understanding of the team's task and suggests implications for how to work together."

We've seen this wisdom in action at Danaher, the $17 billion science and technology company, where the culture is built around continuous improvement. Says Angie Lalor, senior vice president, "Every team here sets stretch goals then tracks metrics on a very regular basis. We put these on what we call Bowler Charts (a nod to the similarity they bear to bowling score grids), which are displayed in each team. The charts have KPIs in red or green—we don't like to use yellow. If a KPI is red, we go through a problem-solving process to get to the root cause and implement counter measures to address it."

This is a process that's seen as positive, exhilarating even. A leader or team with red KPIs doesn't take it personally, but sees it as an intellectual journey to find root causes. "Ninety-nine times out of one hundred it's not going to be related to a person's failure," Lalor said. "Looking at issues like this gives us freedom to be transparent in a safe environment. As a leader, I might have nothing but red on my Bowler Chart, but it's not going to feel like a personal failure. It's going to be an opportunity to find the root causes and counteract them. It injects a level of humility into the organization, which we thrive on."

The lesson we learn here is that no matter what your team does, it's important to choose the right metrics and indicators to judge your success—from product throughput time or supply chain miles, to customer engagement or answer time in a call center, to patient safety or staff churn in a hospital. Looking at the right numbers makes everything less personal and more focused on helping the overall team and bigger organization succeed.

Looking at things from this perspective makes improvement the ultimate goal, and creates tangible ways for a team to prove its worth. Which means if management or customers snort at your key performance indicators (KPIs), then they are either the wrong metrics, or your stakeholders need to be convinced why they are important. This process can even work with creative teams, such as marketing or consulting or teaching, where KPIs might include tracking budget spend or client satisfaction ratings. The bottom line: KPIs must be focused on what we can achieve for the business, and let us know if we are being successful in a very specific time-period—a single shift, a week, or a month. They only work if they provide helpful information the team needs to run its day-to-day operations, and if they make it impossible to hide from failures when they do arise. In contrast, vanity metrics may look good in a press release—number of website hits, for instance—but do little to prove a team's worth.

One last note: When it comes to crafting motivating team goals, there is nothing more powerful than putting the focus solidly, and fervently, on serving customers. A goal-oriented focus on your end-user is an enormously energizing force, because most of us in our working lives take pride, and derive great satisfaction, from helping people improve their lives in some way. That's the focus of our next chapter.

FIVE

NOW, DON'T FORGET YOUR CUSTOMERS

Create Alignment Around Serving Them

With global warming, pollution, hurricanes, and disease, many of the world's ocean reefs are in sorry shape. The iconic Great Barrier Reef, as one example, has seen the worst bleaching event in recorded history. But amid the doom, coral reef conservationist Dr. Joshua Cinner and his research colleagues went searching for bright spots. They looked for reefs that have more fish than expected, those that are thriving in comparison to others with similar challenges.

Contrary to what you might expect, the healthiest reefs they found aren't all in remote places, where humans are absent or fishing is banned. Instead, most are home to lots of people who fish them actively. In these places, humans aren't leaving the coral and fish alone; instead, they are *managing* the reefs responsibly.

On Karkar Island, off the coast of Papua New Guinea, the people here practice what's called marine tenure, where villages can keep neighbors from accessing their part of the reef. They also rotate harvests, closing off sections of reefs for months or years—giving fish time to lose their fear of people, and allowing populations to recover. The result is a thriving ecosystem where people, coral, plants, fish, sharks, and other sea creatures live in an interdependent biodiversity. Fish and turtles keep the coral picked clean and grasses trimmed; the coral and plants provide a refuge from predators for fish; the sharks and humans, in turn, keep more aggressive hunters—like groupers—from overpopulating and decimating herbivore populations.

The point for us: A business team can be a thriving ecosystem of its own, and that's true no matter how diverse a group of people are working together—no matter the differences in age, cultural background, functional expertise, or geographic location. In Chapter 4, we highlighted the benefits of tapping into differences in team member's unique perspectives and expertise by encouraging openness and team debates. Here, we will focus on creating alignment, even in the most diverse of groups.

Getting teams unified around a codified purpose has become an increasingly urgent issue for managers in a time of growing diversity of working populations and globalization of operations. Of course, diversity and globalization can be great benefits: They make teams more aware of, and responsive to, the needs of a wide range of customers. We were reminded of this lately, listening in on a conference call as an employee in Mumbai piped up to remind his teammates that their new product—which was to be bound in leather—might appear top-shelf in their part of the world, but in his corner it would be in bad taste. From design to marketing, customer support to sales, production to purchasing, having members of a team attuned to nuances in cultural preferences and norms is a great help in tailoring products and services to particular constituencies, and in appreciating business opportunities that might otherwise be overlooked.

Procter & Gamble was one of the first companies we saw to actively listen to its diverse workforce to grow its business. As one example, P&G started investing a great deal in America's black community, and began using images of diverse families to market products such as Oil of Olay, Pantene, and Tide that resonated with African-American consumers—to tap better in to their monstrous $1.3 trillion buying power. One ad called 'Nostalgia Dad' featured an African-American man lovingly cradling his sleeping young son. The ad was designed to convey warmth and fatherly caretaking, and the pair's crisp white T-shirts seemed almost peripheral. It also was designed to counter stereotypes of fatherless African-American households. "It was very deliberate to have a man with his son," said Najoh Tita-Reid, associate director of P&G's multicultural marketing unit. "It was very deliberate for him to have a wedding ring on."

The point: More diverse teams can look at issues from different perspectives; and the research shows they can also solve problems better. A study conducted by Katherine Phillips, of the Kellogg School of Management, along with researchers from Brigham Young University and Stanford, found that although people prefer to work in groups in which members are more like themselves, homogeneous groups perform much less well than diverse groups. A particularly interesting aspect of the study was that homogenous groups evaluate their performance more positively than the socially diverse groups that outperform them. It seems comfort with our teammates can be too much of a good thing, though many homogeneous teams tend to be naïve about their limitations.

THE BIRTH OF THE CROSS-FUNCTIONAL TEAM

Leaders often attempt to increase team diversity by building bridges between functions, creating what we call cross-functional teams or interdepartmental work groups with people from around the company, often from around the globe. It's not unusual for tensions to emerge in these teams. Researchers Martine Haas from Wharton, and Mark Mortensen from INSEAD, write about one global team where all the members agreed that serving their client was their goal, but what that meant varied by location. Employees in Norway equated it with providing a product of the absolute highest quality—no matter the cost or time involved. Their colleagues in the United Kingdom, however, felt that if a client needed a solution that was only 75 percent accurate, the less precise solution was fine. Solving this tension required a frank discussion to reach consensus on how the team as a whole defined its objectives.

Tensions like this in the way we work and think about issues are inevitable, yet often are not handled well. Too often leaders assume that cross-functional teams will just magically become the epitome of a healthy business ecosystem—creating synergy between departments that for too long have been at odds as they pursued conflicting goals or subscribed to different beliefs about the right approach to getting their work done.

Unfortunately, members in these new teams frequently remain at odds and never achieve their goals. In a Stanford study we noted earlier, researchers found 75 percent of cross-functional teams have serious operating problems, falling short on at least three of these five performance criteria: "meeting a planned budget; staying on schedule; adhering to specifications; meeting customer expectations; and/or maintaining alignment with the company's corporate goals."

The problem is not completely the fault of employees. Most have been reared in a world where they've been largely siloed from other groups. In their departments, there was often finger-pointing at other functional areas, a lack of understanding of how different groups contributed to the business, and too often a slew of misunderstandings about the real challenges others contended with. We hear software engineers who complain that marketers are clueless about programming constraints and timelines; while marketers tell us engineers have the aesthetic sense of snails. In a hospital, it's not uncommon for Post-op to argue daily with Surgery that they are releasing patients too soon, while Surgery will blame Radiology for holding up images and delaying procedures; meanwhile everyone seems to be mad at the poor Lab.

Employees within these silos have even been reared to vie against their own teammates for resources. They are often incentivized in ways that lead them to compete—taking credit for successes and casting blame toward others for failures. All of a sudden, we ask them to put all this competition aside and work closely together to tackle an important challenge for the company, with no concern for who gets the credit. Wouldn't it be wonderful if human beings were so malleable?

Patty McManus, who's had leadership roles in organizational development with Apple, UC Berkeley, and Kaiser Permanente, notes the common problems that arise on cross-functional teams. She dubs some of these teams the "war zone" type, in which factions form and members maneuver behind the scenes like contestants on *Survivor*. Some leaders may foster this, perhaps relishing in the control it gives them. In these teams, agreement is hardly ever reached. If it is, it's usually undermined soon after.

Then there are teams that really aren't teams, which she calls the unteam type. The only connection members have is to their leader. Meetings are just status updates to the boss and top-down communication. Unless perhaps lunch is provided, get-togethers are seen as pretty much a weekly waste of time for members, helpful only to the boss.

Now, the good news, dysfunction is not inevitable. In our travels, we've met a large number of managers of diverse teams that are really successful. As we've researched their stories, we have found a few best practices to unify teams, of all types, and get them working as thriving ecosystems to align everyone around the mission of serving the customer as the highest priority.

When customer interests rule—really rule—it helps adjudicate between opposing views and interests. For instance, let's say a team tasked with research & development is asked to speed up creation of a new product feature because word has it a competitor has the same thing in the works. Typically, this could involve a protracted tussle over whether the feature can be launched in the timeframe—especially given other demands on R&D. An intense focus on the customer can help broker agreements with various groups involved about any changes that might be required in delivery, assignment of personnel to meet the need, and rescheduling of other work.

Another ancillary benefit is that we've found that a primary focus on serving customers boosts employee engagement by creating clarity about a team's purpose. Helping customers improve their lives in some way is a much stronger motivator to most of us than abstract business goals of increasing sales, bringing down costs, or elevating ROI.

We found a terrific example of this with the Philadelphia 76ers. We've mentioned them a few times in the book, but if you don't follow basketball you might have skimmed over the references. Trust us, this is a great story for everyone. Over the past few seasons, no professional basketball team has had a worse record than the Sixers. In the 2015–2016 season alone, the team won just ten games out of 82. Now imagine having to market this product. The diverse sales group—the majority are not from the Philadelphia area—have taken season ticket sales from 1,700 a year to more than 12,000 over just three seasons. That doesn't happen. In addition, the Sixers have been ranked first in the entire league in new season tickets sold for the last two seasons and second in customer satisfaction.

How did they do all this? They found something that's just as important as winning for their customers: Access.

"The Sixers have done an amazing job," said Joris Drayer, professor of sports marketing at Temple University's school of tourism and hospitality management. "It's easy to sell tickets when the team is amazing," telling the famous story of how the Miami Heat basketball team fired most of its ticket sales staff immediately after signing superstar LeBron James, now with the Cleveland Cavaliers.

Sixers CEO Scott O'Neil said that it's helped his sales team having a coach who is as customer-focused as Brett Brown. Said O'Neil: "One time Coach Brown says, 'I'd like to take the front-row season ticket holders out to dinner. What do you think?'" These are the people paying anywhere from $800 to $1,600 a seat, forty-one times a year, for home games. "I said I think that would be the coolest idea I've heard from a coach in my life. So he takes them out to a fancy dinner and he has each of his coaches walk them through the Xs and Os of how we see our team. It's unbelievable."

Brown next volunteered to meet with other season ticket-holders before each game—no matter where they sit—showing an intimate group of twenty fans at a time the game diagrams, and helping them understand the strategies to contain the opposing team. And this is an hour before the team takes the court, every single game, with a new group each time!

Soon, that kind of customer-focus spread throughout the Sixers. One customer, Derek Koss, talked about how a handful of players and the Sixers' dance team showed up for his son's bar mitzvah. Koss had balked at the price of courtside seats, but now uses them for clients, rewards employees, and treats his children, who sometimes get to go on court and shoot baskets. "The experience at courtside is completely different," he said. "It's almost like a playground game. You hear the grunts, the bickering back and forth."

Said Craig McClure, team lead of member services, "What's led us to so much success is that our reps genuinely believe they are helping people. They aren't reading off a script talking with customers, but they are connecting the dots between what a customer wants and what we have as a team. Are we speaking with a fan or a business customer? How can the person benefit from the product? If it's a father who has a couple of kids, this is going to give him forty-one opportunities to come out to an NBA game and create an experience with his family."

When customers argue they could buy tickets from a reseller, McClure says his reps counter with, "Yeah, but we can get you *access*: We can get your feet on the floor. All our season ticket holders have met Coach Brown an hour before the game, they've all had pictures with players, they've all shot hoops on the court. They feel special."

"Surprise and delights are what we call them," said Jill Snodgrass. "We don't measure results on sales alone, but just as importantly on all the connections our people are able to create with our customers."

FROM ALUMINUM TRUCKS TO FROSTY'S WITH A BLAST

With rising gas prices, customers of the Ford Motor Company were seeking better fuel efficiency, which meant a redesign of the best-selling vehicle in the United States—the F-150 pickup truck. Ford would introduce a new economical six-cylinder engine and, far more radically, rebuild the truck with an all-aluminum body. The F-150 cross-functional team began planning a year-and-a-half before the program kickoff. Pete Reyes was chief engineer for the top-secret project. He said planning the new vehicle was like producing a movie. "Your team conceives it, hammers it out, and hopefully it goes on to a long and prosperous production run," he said.

His big team had within it smaller, parallel teams that took on various aspects of the truck. Together they'd meet monthly for a year and a half, making sure all the pieces would come together into a viable vehicle. "Everybody crossed boundaries, and they came back with a lot of feedback that shaped what we were going to do," he said.

Peter Frantzeskakis and Jerry Farrell served as Reyes' chief lieutenants. "Whether it was marketing or manufacturing, we stuck with common goals," Reyes said. "Peter worked with the technical groups, and Jerry, who used to come in at 5:30 a.m., handled all the deliverables and the work flows. I don't think I'll ever work on a team that tight again. We made all our deadlines."

The team grew to one thousand members strong, and had to overcome unique problems, like the awkward fact that there wasn't enough high-strength, auto-grade aluminum in the world to cover the F-150's volume. "We had to build that supply," Reyes said.

By the delivery date, the truck's fuel economy had increased as much as 29 percent—making the F-150 the most fuel-efficient standard pickup truck ever sold. And the marketplace reaction? By the fall of launch year, Ford's third-quarter earnings were up $1.1 billion from the prior year, largely on sales of this redesigned flagship vehicle.

Another instructional example of customer-focused success comes from Skanska USA. Rich Cavallaro found himself in the early 2010s as the new head of Skanska USA's Civil division. "It was basically seven acquired companies where the leaders got together once a year for half a day of meetings and half a day of golf," he said. "We didn't share people, we didn't share knowledge. We built roads in the northeast and marine in the south. But we didn't do marine anywhere but the south or roads anywhere but the north.

I figured if we could use all of our capabilities for our customers, everywhere we operated, we could win lots of market share."

But getting there would be a challenge. Cavallaro had to convince an entrenched group to work cross-functionally. He started with their wallets. Where each region had a bonus tied to its own performance, over three years he convinced them to adopt a single bonus for the entire business unit—one that would be more lucrative as the large team grew. Another change: He assigned all talent to be owned by the division COO who had a national view, which meant after a job was complete the COO could move people where necessary to help meet pressing customer needs.

Cavallaro admits there were glitches along the way, but over the next few years his group doubled sales—from $1.2 billion to $2.5 billion—as barriers fell in a traditionally siloed business unit. And when Skanska needed a new president and chief executive officer to head up its entire US operations, they turned to the customer-focused team builder Cavallaro.

Today, in his new role, the CEO is most proud to have brought together a team from four functional groups, as well as outside partners, to win the $4 billion renovation of LaGuardia Airport in New York. The bid process took a full two years for the cross-functional team. "We had to get people out of their offices and push them into one office where they started to get to know each other, stopped believing in their functional area, and started focusing on the customer's needs," he said. The result was winning one of the largest construction jobs in American history.

Of course, customer-centric initiatives have been a major emphasis for other businesses as well in recent years. According to research conducted by Deloitte & Touche, companies that are deemed customer-centric are found to be 60 percent more profitable than those that aren't. It's easy to appreciate why when you see intense customer-focus in action.

Take the case of the innovation in customer care recently at The Wendy's Company. Vice President Frank Leary was tasked with helping the organization focus better on customer needs, and formed the Customer Experience team, which is now located smack dab in the middle of the Dublin, Ohio, headquarters. Customers can text, call, use social media, email, send a letter, and soon will be able to use American Sign Language to contact the group. Team members practice a BLAST approach to understanding customer's needs:

- **B**elieve the customer and what they tell us is true
- **L**isten first
- **A**pologize
- **S**atisfy their need
- **T**hank them

"Every person who contacts us has a story," Leary said. "We received a text from a customer recently who said, 'Thanks a lot Wendy's, you messed up my order again.' We texted back, 'So sorry.' We asked what happened and where they were." It was a couple who had just gotten on the freeway and had to travel 59 miles to get home, and the order they'd received was wrong. "We found where they were, and ten miles ahead there was another Wendy's franchisee, owned by a different franchisee. Our team member called and talked to the owner there. We texted back, 'We are going to refund your money and do the order right . . . and add some free Frosty's. Take the Broad Street exit and go right and there's a Wendy's. The manager will take care of you.' A few minutes later we got a response, 'Wow, Wendy's. How did you do that?' "

The customer said that it had been a bad day. He had to take his wife to chemotherapy, and they were on their way home. But, he added, 'You not only made the order right, you brightened our day. Thank you!' "

Imagine the powerful word-of-mouth advertising that the couple—and other customers—has done for the company because of a renewed focus on customer attention. But think also about how proud the team members feel about being able to understand their customers better and focus all their efforts on wowing them.

Much of the attention in the recent literature on enhancing the customer experience has focused on harnessing new technologies, as Wendy's has, but extraordinary focus on serving the customer doesn't just rely on tools. It's fostered by leaders. If you've ever stayed at a Ritz-Carlton, for one example, you'd swear the employees got together to conspire to make your day. Our six-foot-five-inch-tall trainer Chris Kendrick ripped his pants from ankle to thigh ten minutes before going on stage in a Ritz ballroom (he texted us a photo in panic), but thanks to a staff taught to bend over backward in serving guests by their event-team leaders, Chris was wearing a new pair of trousers (courtesy of an equally tall fellow in maintenance) before he stepped into the lights.

How can a manager rally a team like this through a focus on customers? Most of the books and TED-like talks on this topic speak about corporatewide customer service initiatives. We've seen, though, that individual managers can do more to foster more commitment to customers than anyone. And that's true not just for customer-facing teams, such as those answering phones, making sales, or delivering a service, but throughout an organization.

And a great way for managers to do this is to draw on the insights of the growing field of customer-experience research.

KNOW THY CUSTOMERS

The current drive to make companies more customer centric has been propelled, in large part, by the human-centered design movement emerging out of the technology sector. Donald Norman was vice president of the Advanced Technology Group at Apple and now runs a consultancy on the user-experience. He's said that designing products for customers, "is really an act of communication, which means having a deep understanding of the person with whom the designer is communicating." For a team leader, of any team, we could paraphrase that to say that understanding customers better, and keeping their core needs constantly in mind, helps assure that our team members are speaking their language. Norman coined the term *user-experience design*, from which *customer experience* was derived.

The core argument that products and services must be designed with more sensitivity to users is hardly mind-blowing. Accomplishing it, however, is the trick. Human-centered design advocates have developed a few methods that are better at understanding customers' preferences, improving on the traditional methods of focus groups and customer surveys. One of the best ways is to create customer "personas," a term that means profiling individual customers, with specificity about who they are and aspects of their lives that will help employees meet their needs and improve service. Generally, three to five (at the most) of these profiles are created that represent the range of customer groups, by age, buying preferences, or other key differentiators. Perhaps an exercise like this might seem overkill—aren't your customers obvious?—unfortunately, they can be anything but to employees. When we pose the question: "Who do you worry about pleasing?" to groups of workers, we often find that the person they are most worried about is "the boss," or maybe "the doctor" in health care. On manufacturing or engineering teams, employees are frequently confused if their customer is the reseller or the end user or both.

We've seen a number of great teams start to use profiles of their customers to rally employees. An insurance company we visited recently has narrowed things down to four core customer segments—considering age, income, and other needs. They were not represented in generalities, but with a face and a name. Jared was a Millennial, and under his picture was a list of preferences. For instance, he wanted his car insurance and health coverage delivered on an app via a hand-held device; affordability and mobile convenience were his core drivers. Susan was a small-business owner, and she needed comprehensive personal and business coverage—offered up by a trustworthy person in an office located near her. An agent who actually picked up a phone was more important than cost to this Boomer, though she did seek fairly priced services as well as agent expertise.

We've seen personas like these created by teams in all types of industries. Of course, they'll never represent 100 percent of customers. That is unrealistic. But personas can capture enough to help humanize client segments for employees, which is why you always give them names. The profiles typically include de-mographic information—salary, age, job titles, and so on, but also goals and challenges the customer faces, their values and fears, and the best messages to reach them—usually in an elevator pitch format. One best practice is to include some quotes from real cus-tomers alongside these personas.

GET OUT INTO THE WILD

Another way customer-centered teams connect with stakeholders is by getting out and observing people using their products "in the wild." Anyone developing a new product, for example, can learn a great deal about problems with prototypes they've built by observ-ing people trying to use them in their daily lives. This is one reason that software firms alpha, then beta test every new product—and listen carefully to feedback. Great team leaders help their people develop a better understanding of customers, and more empathy for their needs, by taking their teams out to encounter those who use their services, or bringing customers to them if the team is too big or too spread out.

Johnson & Johnson leaders are especially good at this. We saw it firsthand when we were asked to address the Worldwide Pro-curement team not long ago. To close the meeting, leaders had hand-picked a customer to speak for a few minutes to their em-ployees. This well-spoken woman explained how a medicine made by a J&J company successfully treated her father's cancer—which was thought to be terminal. There were more than a few tears shed during her remarks, and at the end she offered her family's sincere thanks to the Procurement team for helping ensure that the materials for vital medicines are sourced and accessible to the patients who need them. This one customer's story made very real the role these professionals play, and the impact they have on patients and their families.

Good managers tell us *what* to do and *how*; great leaders help us see *why* we do what we do for customers.

MAP OUT CUSTOMER INTERACTIONS

Another, eye-opening, way of bringing the customer experience to life is the method of journey mapping—creating a full chart of the interactions customers may have with your team and your organization. A retail store might, for instance, map all of the sorts of conversations and touch-points a customer might have after walking in the door; a call center might do this with a person who dials their order desk.

Take the case of mapping we saw at a midsize bank we visited. This financial institution had a strong culture of divisions. It wasn't isolationism by choice; it was simply how the firm had evolved over time. Each department felt it was functioning at a high level, and you'd have been hard pressed to find a department leader who wouldn't have pegged his or her group in the top quartile for performance. But for some reason—that few of them could have put their fingers on—the company wasn't growing as fast as its peer group. The journey map told a powerful story. Part of the path showed a typical experience for a valued business customer: She started out wanting a commercial loan to expand her inventory, so she made an appointment to see a commercial loan officer downtown. On the way to the meeting, she got a call from the bank's merchant services department (in another part of the country) letting her know that a credit card transaction her business had processed the night before had been rejected. Could she look into it? After the meeting with commercial, on the drive back to her office, she swung by a bank branch to transfer money to her son away in college but the drive-up tellers told her she had to go inside and speak with a "banker" (one of the people in the cubicles) since the transfer was too complex for them. Finally, heading back to the office again, she passed one of the bank's billboards offering low rate mortgage loans. She lamented about not having the time to sit down with a mortgage banker and refinance her house, but thought to herself that she didn't even know where one of the bank's mortgage offices was located.

That's the *Cliff Notes* version. The map provided a visual wealth of information to leaders on how customers' experiences with the bank could be enhanced and its teams interact better together. Any manager with their team can do a version of such a mapping exercise to help employees understand the kinds of problems customers are encountering, and brainstorm ways to serve them better. These visual paths are especially important in helping see the results of the work employees are doing through customers' eyes, helping impress on your people that clients simply don't care about your internal squabbles or divisions of specialty. For customers, it is assumed that when they enter your building, place an order online, call and speak with an employee, or have any kind of direct or indirect interaction with your firm, that it's a united team behind the scenes executing the mission. It is utterly irrelevant to customers that the sales team is having a turf battle with the factory. They are unmoved by the fact that there are delays in shipping because of a miscommunication about product specs between engineering and machining. They can't fathom why radiology would not be in constant communication with their surgeon. Or why a bank can't provide a one-stop experience to help with all their needs. For customers, an organization is a single entity. It is one big team, and as such, the members naturally should work and respond with one accord.

FOCUS MICROBATTLES ON CUSTOMER SEGMENTS

Traditional bureaucratic structures have distanced so much of the work force from real customers. When companies are young and scrappy, the ones that are successful typically have a laser-like focus on serving customers—especially underserved segments, says James Allen, a global strategy leader at Bain & Co.

Startups, the ones that make it, excel in monitoring customer responses and experimenting with changes to products and services to better serve them. "But as companies get big and more bureaucratic," highlights Allen, "internal issues often steal attention from interactions with the customer. Senior executives spend more time optimizing functions and negotiating among them. Innovation gets handled centrally, far from the front line. Customers are neither involved nor welcome. And growth slows or grinds to a halt."

To combat this, team leaders can craft goals for their teams tied specifically to customer segments. Allen advises cross-functional teams be formed that are tasked with what he calls microbattles—discrete, customer-focused initiatives to improve results. Take the case of a sales group. The Bain leader points out that most sales teams will have revenue targets rolled up by geography, category, brand, or product—for instance, "Grow sales of gardening equipment on the West Coast by 4 percent." In contrast, a microbattle would more specifically define the goals as "Win a 50 percent share in Southern California's do-it-yourself gardener business in cooperative hardware chains by displacing Bad Trimmer Co." This goal points more specifically to a particular type of customer in a more circumscribed area and includes important information about the kind of stores they like to shop in and what entrenched competitor the team needs to beat.

REINVENT YOURSELF

It is important to remember that every one of the great teams and organizations we've studied has had to *reinvent* itself to ensure that their people work more cross-functionally and are unified around an understanding of customer needs. Those who've had to visit Mayo Clinic will tell you the experience is nothing like most health care visits. Redesigned to deliver what is called "destination medicine," experts from a range of specialties now work as codified teams to diagnose and treat very serious cases. And because they know that coming to Minnesota is usually a family affair, Mayo has redesigned its exam rooms to accommodate large, fluid groups of well-wishers. The sofas can be expanded to seat half a dozen people at once. All of this puts "the needs of the patient," as Mayo's motto puts it—at the center of the experience.

As effective as Mayo's customer experience can be, it wasn't born to be so collaborative, they had to turn their focus from departments to customers. Likewise have many of the best organizations and teams we've studied. The terrific IKEA product design process now brings together team members with backgrounds in design, sourcing, shipping, manufacturing, and customer insight into long-lasting teams that do extraordinary work.

A final example comes from an unlikely source, the Museum of Modern Art (MoMA) in New York, home to works of art from Pablo Picasso's *"Les Demoiselles d'Avignon"* to Andy Warhol's *Gold Marilyn Monroe*. A little background you may not be aware of, museums can sometimes be among the most insulated of institutions, with departments often operating like their own museums. Even within a department, the art of one period (Middle Ages, say) might be curated separate from the next period (the Renaissance).

So, eyebrows were raised when the MoMA announced in the fall of 2016 that it had published one of the most monumental, comprehensive online histories ever made available to researchers, artists, curators, and the public. Michelle Elligott, chief of archives, and Fiona Romeo, director of digital content and strategy, led a cross-functional team of archivists who worked together for two and a half years to break down department boundaries and integrate tens of thousands of folders worth of exhibitions to create what they called a "living archive."

Consider this art initiative from a customer's point of view. They don't care that many museums can be siloed, they probably aren't even aware of it. Most don't care how this online archive came together. They expect the experience of attending this wonderful museum or going online and learning more about its exhibitions to be a homogenous event. And now, researching all activities that have happened at the museum are unified, as if narrated by a single voice.

And so it is with your team and your customers. They have every right to assume that the opinions, products, or services of one team member is united with the entire organization—all focused on their needs.

Is it too much for them to ask to never be forgotten?

WHO LEFT THE GATE OPEN?

What We Can Learn from the Fall of Constantinople

E arly in the year 1452, there arrived in the great city of Constantinople a Hungarian by the name of Orban.

The man possessed a rarified skill in the mid-fifteenth century—he could build cannons—and he offered his talent in casting these large bronze guns to the Byzantine Emperor, Constantine XI. The emperor was certainly intrigued. With the Turkish Ottomans threatening to invade, Orban would be a good man to have on the payroll; so the emperor authorized a tiny stipend be paid to keep the cannon founder in the city.

Orban set up shop and eagerly went to work, but it was soon clear things would not be as promised. His wages, meager as they were, did not arrive consistently. Promised resources never materialized. He sought audiences with the emperor, but the great man could not find a moment to spare. The luckless canon maker felt unwanted, unappreciated, and finally packed his tools, slipped out of the city, and made his way West—hoping to meet Sultan Mehmet II, the newly crowned, twenty-one-year-old ruler of the Ottoman Empire.

The sultan, although young, was no one's fool. He welcomed the Hungarian courteously. He provided the craftsman with food, clothes, and shelter, then interviewed him carefully. Mehmet asked if he could cast a cannon large enough to smash the walls of Constantinople, the most heavily fortified city in the world.

Orban nodded. "I can shatter to dust not only these walls with the stones from my gun but the very walls of Babylon itself," he said.

Mehmet hired the man on the spot, providing him with wages, but also with all the support he needed to thrive in his craft. Orban, in turn, was good to his word. He built a series of weapons the world had never seen, including one massive cannon thirty-feet long. Mehmet was thrilled with the work, and showered attention and praise on the Hungarian.

On April 6, 1453, the Turkish army arrived at the walls of Constantinople with Orban's guns, where for fifty-three days Mehmet besieged the city—the big cannons steadily narrowing the mighty defenses.

Then, shortly after midnight on May 29, the sultan ordered one last all-out offensive. His troops managed to breach the main walls, but the Byzantines pushed them back. Just when it seemed Constantinople might never fall, a Turkish flag was seen flying near a small postern gate. It seemed the gate had been left open by defenders who had sortied out to attack the flank of the Turkish army. A handful of the sultan's men had pushed through the unlocked entrance, and now more of his warriors were streaming through. Soon the city was overrun.

Mehmet had his prize, which he renamed Istanbul. And so came to an end the great city of Constantinople—all because someone left the gate open *and* because an unappreciated cannon maker slipped through his fingers.

By all accounts, Constantine XI, steward of the most secure fortress in the world, was not a bad man, not at all. He was just busy. He was a manager, after all, and like every other leader he had a thousand demands on his time. It wasn't callousness or hubris or arrogance that brought down his city. He had just been too busy to make a talented cannon maker feel valued; and certainly didn't have the time to spend getting his lowly gatekeepers to understand their roles.

Fast-forward almost six hundred years. Leading a team has not gotten any easier; in fact, it's never been harder. We are not only facing increasing market volatility, uncertainty, complexity, and ambiguity, but the composition of teams is changing rapidly: Members can come from a wide range of cultures and be flung far around the globe, some work full-time while others are temporary, all the while our teams have increased demands for rapid innovation, more cross-functional collaboration, and higher productivity. While technology has handed team leads more powerful tools for communication and analysis, those leaders we meet feel their time is still overtaxed just keeping up with the flood of emails and fire-fighting the latest problems. Working on their own deliverables and reporting to higher management tend to take precedence over inspiring their people. But there is an important lesson for all managers in the fall of Constantinople. Too many are leaving the gate open by not focusing in the right ways on their team members.

No matter what technological tools team leaders may use, no

matter how rich the data they have to inform product development or customer service, the greatest payoffs in performance will come from applying effective soft disciplines to people management.

Think again about Google, one of the world's leading technology innovators—a company driven by the mission of using technology to solve problems better, faster, smarter. If this company, brimming with left-brain engineers and programmers no less, concludes after five years of intensive study that *the* most important factor differentiating high performance teams from average is the use of soft-disciplines by managers, then perhaps it's time for us all to give this more attention.

We are keenly aware of how pressed managers are for time, which is why we have worked hard in writing this book to cull from the best science and from the hands-on experience of some terrific people-managers. Inevitably, some of the specific practices we've recommended will be more appropriate, or more appealing, for some readers than others. That's understandable. Every manager should tailor how they execute on these five disciplines within their own personal styles, the specific composition of their teams, and their work demands.

We recommend bringing your own creativity and voice to these practices, as so many of the managers we've profiled have done. For instance, while one team leader may prefer to have career discussions in the office, another might choose to get out and conduct them more informally by walking and talking with her employees. We've seen formal debates conducted on stage in front of others for a demonstration, while other managers prefer less-structured, free-flowing discussions. Appointing a more senior team member to mentor new arrivals may appeal to some managers, while others may encourage new team members to mentor each other in innovative ways.

Variations on the themes we've presented, and experimentation with specific approaches, is absolutely essential. The only thing we strongly recommend is that managers do seriously consider *how* to best implement each of the five disciplines: Addressing generational differences; managing one-on-one; getting people and teams up to speed faster; fostering psychological safety to speak up, debate, and innovate; and never, ever forgetting customers. We have found improvements in team cohesiveness, collaborative creativity, work engagement, and overall performance will follow.

In today's fiercely competitive business environment, can any leader really afford not to make use of these disciplines to build their teams? After all, the simple truth is, in the end, it's the best team that wins.

PART II

THE LEADER'S TOOLKIT

101 WAYS TO INSPIRE YOUR TEAM

Small Ideas That Drive Big Results

The 101 ideas that follow were gleaned from our research into high-performance teams and from many of our interviews with managers we've met. Knowing your team like you do, you'll be able to decide which will work in your culture and which might not. The idea is not to try them all, but a few you believe might work in your culture.

As always, with these kinds of lists, we encourage an open mind. You might come across a few that could cause a spontaneous eye roll. That's fine, those probably won't work in your team, but they might in someone else's. With that said, we do suggest breaking out of your typical comfort zone.

And so, we present 101 ways to inspire your team:

1. **KEEP REMOTE PEOPLE FOCUSED.** With remote employees, managers must be more focused on goals and outcomes than

hours clocked. Carrie McKeegan, co-founder of tax preparation company, Greenback, says she uses regular updates and quarterly goal-setting to motivate her team of remote workers. McKeegan relies on two key ways to measure their productivity: Weekly she gets an update about their accomplishments during the week and their focus for the following week, quarterly she works with them on goals to help each stretch and stay focused and productive. **ACTION**: Add weekly one-on-one updates and quarterly goal-setting to better focus your remote employees (as well as everyone else on your team).

2. **LEARN THEIR STORIES**: General Norman Schwarzkopf once said, "I have seen leaders who stood in front of a platoon and all they saw was a platoon. But great leaders see it as forty-four individuals, each of whom has aspirations, each of whom wants to live, each of whom wants to do good." Great leaders make an effort to get to know the individuals on their team one-by-one. **ACTION**: Over the next week, sit down with each of your direct reports for fifteen minutes and learn their story—ask about the person's background, and their hopes and goals for the future. Take notes.

3. **FIND THEIR FLOW.** One of the most deeply satisfying human psychological states is called *flow*. It occurs when a person is so immersed in an activity that he or she loses track of time. The more flow in our jobs, the more happiness we typically feel. **ACTION**: Take a few minutes with each of your people this week to identify the most satisfying conditions of their work, the activities that fuel their passions. Determine if you might be able to incorporate more of these tasks into their work.

4. **RECOGNIZE YOUR MVPS.** Jake Reynolds, senior vice president of ticket sales and service at the Philadelphia 76ers, has each team he oversees present a weekly Team MVP award—voted for by fellow employees. The Team MVP gets a unique rotating award valued by that team (from a golden boot to a wrestling belt). Then, from the group of Team MVPs, an overall MVP is chosen for Reynold's entire ticket sales and service department, and that person receives another rotating award—this one a hard hat signed by all past winners and the basketball team's coach. The awards are handed out every week, without fail, and the entire group gathers to see who is being recognized. Said Jill Snodgrass, vice president, "We tell a story through the MVP awards. If a team has just gone through season ticket renewals, which is a grind, we might give that team a spotlight. Other times the MVP might be someone who's been a great teammate, or someone who hasn't had a lot of sales but is hustling—following the process, doing the dirty work." This kind of storytelling during recognition celebrations helps show everyone that their efforts are noticed, and the behaviors that are valued. **ACTION**: Start giving out a weekly award to help recognize teammates who excel, and those who do the so-called dirty work.

5. **DEFINE YOUR PURPOSE.** Robert Frank, economics professor at Cornell University, said one of the most important dimensions of job happiness is how a person feels about his or her team or organization mission. In short, when people leave work each day, do they feel they have made the world better in some way, or at the very least haven't made it worse. **ACTION**: You might not be able to influence the bigger company

mission, but you can gather your people this week to define a team purpose. If you've already got a team purpose or rally cry, then get together to talk about what it means in your day-to-day work: Are you living it? Where is the team falling short? What could you all do better?

6. **BETTER ALLOCATE YOUR TIME.** The modern world is making managers more, not less, relevant. Harvard Business School professor David Garvin and researcher Lynn Levesque studied managers in retail stores, finding the most effective spend most their time not on logistics or customers, but with employees. They put the right people together on the right shifts and the right teams—assembling groups that could work well together and moving people as necessary; develop each person's career individually; and deal with inevitable personality conflicts that come up. Garvin said the key to managers' success is how well they motivate employees. "My job is to get my managers and associates excited," one high-performing Staples store manager told them. **ACTION:** Today, conduct an inventory of where you spend your time. Is it with your employees, customers, bosses, or on paperwork?

7. **SEND DAILY UPDATES.** DreamWorks Animation CEO Jeffrey Katzenberg generates a tremendous sense of transparency and trust with his daily emails that update the company's 2,100 employees on people he's meeting and conversations he's having. "We didn't expect that simple email could create the organizational glue that bonded people together in ways that we didn't even realize was needed," said Dan Satterthwaite, head of HR. "People discuss it. Based on our annual

employee survey, our employees feel more engaged and connected." **ACTION**: Give this idea a try. During the coming week, be much more open with your team about what you are up to in your meetings and other activities. At the end of the week, ask for feedback from your team members. Has anyone noticed a change? Is it for the better?

8. **UNDERSTAND THE ALLURE.** Great leaders help employees understand what their customers find attractive about rivals and their products: Often openly displaying their competitors' wares in their break rooms or war rooms and encouraging everyone to spend some time to identify the key selling points. By understanding *why* a competitor's offerings might be attractive to a customer, team members are then able to suggest refinements to their own services. **ACTION**: Find a way this week to help employees better understand your competitors' wares and, more important, lead your team in a discussion about how to outpace those rivals.

9. **REPEAT PURPOSE UNPREDICTABLY.** Dan Helfrich, an executive with Deloitte, believes that teams become aligned around purpose; but, he told us, that comes from repetition that is not predictable. "As a leader, you do those little things to embed your purpose but not in a cadence that becomes rote. One week, I might write an email or send out a blog to my team, but they are unpredictable in their cadence and format. Another week, I might do a podcast or send a one-paragraph note to everyone. Yet another week, I might send out a thought of the day, or maybe I'll hold a recognition ceremony to reward someone for living the purpose." **ACTION**: Put together a chart and consider what you can do to shake

up the way you communicate your team's purpose every week.

10. **CREATE A KINDNESS FUND.** Kim Boerema, chief operating officer of California Pizza Kitchen, told us his organization has a core goal of kindness—to their guests, communities, and especially employees. "We have a Kindness Fund," he said. "It's funded by employees to help their fellow teammates in times of financial hardship, if they have needs for their family during tragedies, medical emergencies, and other crises." Employee participation in the fund has gone from 10 percent three years ago to more than two-thirds of employees now contributing to help their own. CPK teams also strive to help others in the community. "Yesterday, we provided a free lunch on Veterans Day, something we do annually, to support our nation's veterans and active duty military," said Boerema. "We also let our teams decide what to do from a kindness perspective in their communities, and they are empowered to pursue their passions and make a difference. It all matters when it comes to giving back to our people and our communities. It is our job as leaders to find out what matters to our team members and help them pursue what matters most to them." **ACTION**: Consider what your team can do to help each other or your community. Put a plan in place this month to give back in some fashion.

11. **NEWBIES ONBOARDING NEWBIES.** A great practice we've seen is asking a new employee to create a how-to video on an important process to put on your intranet, or at the very least, show to other new people when they come on board. The three-to-four minute videos provide the information needed

to get started and be successful at a specific activity. Asking a new person to tackle this project will help them learn and grow and lead them to ask more experienced people on the team for help. **ACTION**: Assign a new hire to put one processes or task into video form this week.

12. **FIND NEW IDEAS.** Quicken Loans has a companywide initiative to find incredible concepts, empowering team members to impact the business. Team members submit their ideas and are then selected to present them in front of a live audience of colleagues while the rest of the company watches on a live broadcast. Those voted with the best ideas receive a paid vacation with their significant other, as well as the opportunity to implement the idea; while runners-up each receive $500 gift cards. **ACTION**: Hold a concept contest in your team this month, with prizes for the best ideas.

13. **INVOLVE MILLENNIALS IN EVENTS.** John Lowery, president of Applied Imaging, says company meetings are a great time to help Millennials feel welcome and included. For one summer gathering, Lowery invited a group of his Millennials who own old Volkswagen vans to display their vehicles. He suggested the meeting have a 1960s theme, and everyone came dressed as hippies and got henna tattoos. Employees were encouraged to Show Their Own Tattoo (as long as it wasn't in a crazy spot). "It was an absolute blast," said Lowery. "For our Millennials, it drew them into a company meeting with fun, but they also felt important and that we were listening. For our Boomers, they dug the fact we were back in the 1960s." **ACTION**: Ask a group of your Millennials to help make your next get-together more inclusive and hip.

14. **A ROSE BY ANY OTHER NAME.** When Dan Johnson took over as CEO of Innovation Credit Union in Saskatchewan, Canada, he asked members (their customers) what they needed. "They told us they want us to be more mobile, very responsive, and able to offer good advice and guidance," Johnson said. The first step was to include this feedback into the organization's vision and mission, and then focus on more subtle items, like titles, to help team members think about the services they offered in new ways. Branches became advice centers, and tellers became member service representatives, clerks became analysts. "A name makes a difference," he said. "If you go to work as a clerk you work in one way, but if you are an analysist you also seek out ways to improve and solve problems. It changes your attitude." **ACTION:** Can you change your team name or some job titles to better fit the needs of your customers?

15. **CREATE A CRISIS.** Scott Weisberg, chief people officer of Wendy's, told us that, even if team leaders aren't going through a crisis, sometimes they have to create one to have their people think differently. Weisberg recalls a leader early in his career, the head of supply chain for another large employer, "Who would pose questions to us, like 'What if we spun off supply chain from our firm and we were Supply Company?' We'd chase that idea and it led to a bunch of productivity. He didn't want to spin us off, but the ideas we came up with made us better." **ACTION:** If you aren't facing a crisis, consider what challenging question you could pose to your team to push their thinking.

16. **AN HOUR A DAY.** When he was president of Texas Health

Presbyterian Hospital Dallas, CEO Britt Berrett instituted a policy called Sacred 60, one hour each day during which team leaders had to be out rounding with their staff. As a result, engagement increased by more than 30 percentage points over the next few years. Of the practice, one manager said, "We're not supposed to be on email or phone, we use the time to ask (our people), 'How's everything going? Is there something that I can do for you? Are there any barriers that are making your job harder?'" **ACTION**: Set aside the same hour every day this week to silence your phone, turn off your computer, and get out and connect with your team.

17. **DEFINE WOW.** Leadership author Ken Blanchard tells of a Department of Motor Vehicles location that was recharged by a new director. Expecting a three-hour labor of pain when he went in, Blanchard was shocked to be in and out in nine minutes. He asked the employees what was different; they said: "Our manager." His desk was in the middle of the main floor, not in a walled office. When Blanchard spoke to the manager, he said: "My job is to reorganize the department on a moment-to-moment basis depending on citizens' needs." As such, he had crossed-trained every employee on everyone else's job, so that they could switch positions when needed to help with backlogs in certain areas. They also had changed their lunch times so everyone was there from 11:30 to 2:00, when things were the busiest. He'd created a place in which customers were valued, and employees felt a greater sense of purpose and drive. **ACTION**: Ask yourself: Does every employee on my team have a clear focus on our customers?

How can you better define for your team what customers need and what wowing a customer looks like?

18. **CELEBRATE SMALL WINS.** A sales rep finally schedules a discovery meeting at a hard-to-reach account, a new hire turns around her first angry customer, the technology team pushes out an update ahead of time. Not all celebrations need to be for huge wins. At LevelEleven, enterprise account executive Brendan Hartt said, "We love playing 'small ball' and celebrating the assists, singles, and doubles. It's not uncommon for our team to recognize each other with a few dozen Timbits from Tim Hortons following a prospecting day. We send out emails following a 'closed-won' opportunity with the subject line 'Score – New Deal won at XYZ company for __ users.' He said the resulting blow-back recognition that follows is even better than the original missive, as acknowledgement from peers, management, and a few attached GIFs get everyone pumped up. **ACTION**: When was the last time you recognized a small victory with a blast email? If it's been more than a few days, it's time today.

19. **EMPOWER YOUR TEAM.** There's a difference between empowered employees and an empowered team. An empowered individual has authority to make decisions alone, rather than needing approval or instructions from a manager. In an empowered team, however, each teammate has a voice in group decisions and the collective team may make changes in how they do business to best serve customers. An organization structured around empowered teams is a powerful force. **ACTION**: Consider if you have a handful of empowered people

on your team who you trust, or does your entire group act like an empowered team?

20. **KICK OUT SPECTATORS.** On high performance teams, it's an expectation that everyone in a meeting is an essential participant. Spectators are not welcome. Ken Segall worked closely with Apple for years as its ad agency creative director. He learned the following on how to hold a great meeting: Throw out the least necessary person at the table, walk out if it lasts more than thirty minutes, and do something productive during the day to make up for the time you spent in the meeting. **ACTION**: For your next meeting, ask yourself if anyone at the table might be unnecessary. If they shouldn't be there, instead of kicking them out, several times push them to speak up and offer their opinion.

21. **USE A COLLABORATION APP.** Salesforce.com's internal team members collaborate by sharing ideas via a social networking application. On the app, employees upload data to analyze, compare drafts of documents, and share ideas in real time, eliminating the lag associated with email and other methods of communication. **ACTION**: Implement a team collaboration tool to help your team share and communicate more effectively.

22. **THANK ALL APPLICANTS.** KimArie Yowell, Quicken Loans senior director of talent development, told us it's important to begin the new hire onboarding process the moment a person fills out a job application. "Every single candidate who applies to Quicken Loans gets a phone call," she said, "even if we don't have a position or they might not be a fit. There

are no exceptions, no excuses to this rule. We want you to feel valued." She noted that one current Quicken Loans teammate had applied seventy-seven times (and received seventy-seven friendly phone calls) before finally getting the nod on the seventy-eighth attempt. "She is now with the company, and is a go-getter who is making an impact every single day. That's tenacity." **ACTION**: Starting with your very next hire, thank everyone who applies with a personal phone call, whether they get the job or not.

23. **PRACTICE EXTREME OPENNESS.** Moz company founder and CEO Rand Fishkin is extremely open with his employees. When he proposed to his wife, he posted about it that night on the company blog. He's even disclosed his personal finances to employees. However, the most extreme instance of Fishkin's radical honesty is in his detailed account of his failure to secure a $24 million venture capital deal for the firm. Part of Moz's values include the statement, "We will share the inner workings of our company—both the good and bad—openly," and Fishkin is a living embodiment. **ACTION**: Open up and be vulnerable with your team about something important in this week's team meeting.

24. **INVOLVE OTHERS IN MAKING DECISIONS.** To encourage collaboration in the cockpit, the airline industry has developed ways to have pilots debate every decision. In speaking with Broc King, a first officer with Southwest Airlines, he told us pilots today use a process called Crew Resource Management to deliberate decisions and reach consensus using all available input, procedures, policies, and system knowledge. "Say that we were approaching a big thunderstorm," he told us. "It

might be evident the way we should go, but the captain has been trained that he'll ask me, 'What do you think?' He'll listen to what I have to say and together we come up with a conclusion." **ACTION**: Consider the biggest decision you are facing right now. Get a couple of employees together today to brainstorm potential solutions.

25. **FIND THE RIGHT FIT.** Toby Dodd is executive managing director of global occupier services for Cushman & Wakefield, a 45,000 employee firm that specializes in commercial real estate services. He is a believer that someone who might not be the best fit in your team might be successful somewhere else. "Generally people know if they are underperforming on a team," he said. "And as a result, other team members end up suffering and eventually blame leadership. When we move underperformers to another area or team, my experience is everyone is happier and more successful. People may think you are being unkind, but you are being unkind if you keep them in place. We always consider how to find a win-win solution for the individual and team." **ACTION**: This may be hard, but is there someone on your team who is hurting your team culture? Can you find a way to deal compassionately but firmly with the situation?

26. **THREE WINS A DAY.** At closing time, Philadelphia 76ers sales team employees are asked to send a daily email with their 3 Wins of the Day. These may not necessarily be sales they've made, but could be good conversations, perhaps helping another associate learn a task, or how they worked the sales process. "That way we are recognizing the intangibles every day," said Jake Robinson, director of group sales. "It's all

positive, even if you haven't made a sale for a while." The manager responds to each rep that evening. "He'll praise efforts and might forward his response to the whole team," added Robinson. And this, he says, is especially good for new employees and those who are struggling. **ACTION**: Ask your team members to email you their three biggest victories of the day for just one week and see what happens.

27. **FIND TEAM PLAYERS.** In Wiley Cerilli's sales team at SinglePlatform, he's discovered a few shortcuts that help him hire the right people. "It's pretty obvious to us whether someone's going to be the right fit for our culture, just as how often the word *I* comes up in your interview with them, versus how often they talk about their team and how many team members' names come up," Cerilli said. **ACTION**: To gauge an applicant's approach to teamwork, start asking probing questions such as: What do you think about prior to your first meeting with a new team you'll be a part of? What's your strategy if you disagree with the direction the team is taking on solving a problem? Can you be a good team player and disagree with your manager?

28. **CONNECT WITH CUSTOMERS.** The LEGO Group company never loses sight of its ultimate goal—to entertain and promote creativity in children. That's why, each week, Lego brings in a new group of kids to play with new potential products. Employees are then given real-time feedback on the changing preferences of their target audience. **ACTION**: While your team might not be able to invite end users to provide real-time feedback on your products, ask yourself when was the last time you and your people interviewed customers about

their needs from your team, what they like about your products or services, and what frustrates them?

29. **UNDERSTAND CHALLENGES.** At one large healthcare company we visited, the CEO had recently spent a day blindfolded to understand better the world of a recently hired visually impaired employee. It not only helped the leader appreciate the potential challenges faced by that individual, but gave him an appreciation of the abilities and resolve that the person brought to the organization. **ACTION**: Ask yourself if there is there something more I can do to appreciate the perspective and differences of my team members?

30. **START WITH *YES*.** One of the basic tenets of improvisational comedy is to start with "yes"—and even more specifically with "yes and." Mark Chapman, customer fulfillment director with Tesco, believes team leaders should start with *yes*, and work their way back to *how*. For instance, "If a cashier asks for Saturday off, the reaction used to be 'You can't because . . .' Now, we start with yes," he said. "It might just be one Saturday. We ask them to do what's important for us: Smile at every customer, ask for the Club Card. It doesn't translate if we don't care about what's important to them. Now, if the same person comes in three weeks on the trot looking for Saturday off, then it's a different conversation. We might not be able to do it, but we can treat each other like adults." **ACTION**: Start with *yes* the next time one of your employees has a request. And, even if you absolutely can't agree, carefully consider the request and help the person feel heard and respected and brainstorm other solutions together.

31. **INVITE HONESTY.** Many leaders say they have an open-door policy, but how many truly push their people to give them honest feedback? Quicken Loans CEO Bill Emerson conducts face-to-face meetings over lunch, every month, with a different group of about twenty team members. The three-hour meetings are no-holds-barred discussions with no formal agenda. The employees get to know Emerson better, and pretty soon they are talking about their roles and offering up ideas on how to improve the company—from little things to the big picture. **ACTION**: Take a group of employees you normally might not spend much time with out to lunch this week and ask for their honest feedback about how things are going in their worlds. If you don't learn something new, you aren't asking the right questions.

32. **TEAM UP TO SERVE.** John Lowery, president of Applied Imaging, has built cross-functional unity by encouraging his people to serve within the community as teams during work hours—and he pays them to do it. However, there is one caveat, each employee has to pick people from other functional areas to work with. For instance, a salesperson has to choose someone from administration and someone from technical for their team, and so on. "When you spend time like this together, you see the other person as human," said Lowery. "They spend time together serving in the community, and you know what, they develop a nonbusiness relationship. This breaks down barriers that might exist at work and helps to build a team. We've found the next time they interface at work, the relationship developed outside our company has a positive impact on the relationship they need to help

each other inside the company." **ACTION**: Figure out a way this week to encourage your people to volunteer or work cross-functionally like this.

33. **ADOPT AN AFTERNOON LIFT.** One of our favorite examples of teambuilding we saw in a product design work group a few years ago at Microsoft. Each day, one person signed up to blast a song across the work area at three o'clock. Everyone was dragging by that point and needed a lift. Some people got up and danced, and everyone clapped when the song was done. Classics *Mustang Sally*, *Born to Be Wild*, and *Living on a Prayer* were a few popular choices. It was clear to us that solid relationships were in place before this kind of fun could be accepted and authentic. **ACTION**: Figure out a daily ritual that your team can adopt to restore energy levels later in the day.

34. **HIRE FOR CULTURE FIT.** Amy Miller, founder of the franchise Amy's Ice Cream, stopped giving out formal job applications to potential teammates. Instead, she and her team now hand out paper bags. "You are asked to do something creative with it while including at least your name and phone number," Miller said. One bag came back attached to a helium balloon, made to look like the basket of a hot-air balloon, another applicant turned the bag into an aquarium complete with live goldfish, one pasted pictures of her accomplishments on the outside. "The application bag is pretty effective at weeding out applicants who probably wouldn't fit into the company culture," she says. **ACTION**: Implement a creative way to bring the right people into your team.

35. **TEACH WHILE HAVING FUN.** During Engineering Week at Pella

Corporation, makers of windows, employees and their families were invited to enjoy an event at the Science Center in Des Moines, which included a booth where kids were encouraged to try to break a window by hitting a baseball through it. There was a method to the madness: The window was made of hurricane glass, which can break, but will not shatter; and while the children (and many grownups) were batting, everyone was learning about the product's advantages. **ACTION**: Ask yourself: How can we incorporate a product knowledge quiz or demonstration into our next team-building activity?

36. **PLAY TOGETHER.** Since football (soccer) is a global sport and, since Bain & Company is a global firm, each year since 1987 a different city has hosted the Bain World Cup tournament. More than 1,200 employees of all abilities from around the world now come to play, bringing out their inner Messi and Neymar during the three-day competitions. Bain also has a rock band in each of its locations, so team members can jam and perform together. **ACTION**: Bring your team together outside of work hours in a bowling, softball, Frisbee golf, or soccer league, maybe run a Ragnar (long-distance run) together, or do another fun team activity. We highly recommend you choose something that you—as the leader—*aren't* good at (otherwise it's not as much fun for the team).

37. **BUILD YOUR HOME TEAM.** Most leaders have teams at home too—their families—and they need to remember that their young home-team members (kids) are going to mess up. Kids will make you sick with worry, won't make their beds, will torment siblings, will refuse to shower, will shower too much, will take your money, and lie about it! Still, don't blow a fuse.

Remember, you did this stuff. **ACTION**: Dig way down deep and conjure up a smile for your kids the next time they mess up. It may feel counterintuitive, but what's done is done, so what good is raging like a college basketball coach?

38. **SPARK HEALTHY DEBATES.** In great team cultures, leaders take the time to let differing opinions bubble to the surface—realizing that members sometimes have to argue things out a little. Now, we don't mean Mr. Spock and Captain Kirk fighting to the death with a Vulcan Lirpa, but disagreeing in civil, yet spirited discussions where participants want only what's best for the end user. **ACTION**: Recall the last time your team engaged in a healthy work debate. If it's been more than a few weeks, ask your staff, "Why don't we debate?" Try to identify the root cause.

39. **SHUT OFF ON VACATION.** Time off is time off, after all. There are no deadlines, no meetings, and no numbers to run when you are on the beach or the rollercoaster. When you turn off your phone and computer, you also teach your employees that it's okay for them to decompress in their time away. **ACTION**: Shut off completely on your next vacation. And while you're at it, surprise your significant other (or kids) by relaxing on airplanes (there are going to be delays), and lightening up in traffic.

40. **REWARD SUCCESSES AND FAILURES.** Genentech celebrates everyday efforts at its Ho-Ho Gatherings—regular Friday afternoon social events where employees and leaders often dress in crazy outfits. Key successes (like the launch of a new medicine) are honored by an all-employee bell ringing. The company even celebrates smart risks that didn't work

out with its Awesome Failure Awards—knowing that such efforts will help fuel future innovation. **ACTION**: Ask yourself: What informal and formal awards could our team introduce to reinforce what matters most?

41. **FACILITATE MENTORING.** At KPMG, mentoring initiatives are available to all employees. More than 12,300 of its employees and partners are engaged in these mentoring relationships, and leaders believe their mentoring program is one of the keys to keeping great people. We love this: Each year, the firms hold a National Mentoring Awards program to recognize the contributions of exceptional mentors in driving the success of its people. **ACTION**: Connect a few of your people today with mentors in other areas of the organization. After a few months, find a way to publicly thank those mentors.

42. **LIFT STRUGGLERS.** Jack Welch, retired chairman and CEO of General Electric, and Suzy Welch, former editor-in-chief of the *Harvard Business Review*, write about the connection between recognition and success: "We often ask audiences if they think their companies celebrate success enough, and typically no more than 10 percent of the crowd says yes. What a lost opportunity. Celebrating victories along the way is an amazingly effective way to keep people engaged on the whole journey. And we're not talking about celebrating just the big wins." Recognition of small and big achievements not only helps fuel team pride, but helps people think of themselves differently—as winners. Remember, however, that people who need cheering the most are often those who are struggling. **ACTION**: Consider who on your team needs a lift and today find a way to publicly recognize them for

something they are doing well (even if everything in their performance is not perfect).

43. **IDENTIFY YOUR HEROES.** One great ice-breaking exercise for your team involves asking each person to write down three of their heroes—doesn't matter if it's a historical figure or their mother. Next, have them list the characteristics they most admire about those people. A facilitator then can create a running list of the most common characteristics of the admired individuals of the team. It's a terrific way to help people understand more about each other, and is the start of creating a list of team values or ground rules. **ACTION**: Find an hour this week for this exercise.

44. **CHECK OUT THE COMPETITION.** We've seen leaders send team members to shop their competition in-person, especially those in service or retail jobs. Managers might give everyone a little cash to spend with their rivals, or just ask employees to browse, and everyone reports back and shares what they learned, especially the positives. A variation is to visit a vendor that sells your product side-by-side with the competition and see what the sales people say about each. An alternative: Employees anonymously visit their own company and evaluate their products and services. **ACTION**: This week, work with your employees to find a way to check out the competition (even if it's online), and use that new knowledge to better understand how to beat them.

45. **START A LETTER-WRITING CAMPAIGN.** We often ask groups of leaders if they've received a handwritten thank you note from a boss or colleague and if they've kept it. It's amazing how many tell us they've kept these missives for years.

ACTION: Give each team member a stack of thank-you cards, and ask them to start recognizing their coworkers—using specific language tied to your team values—when they see someone doing something great. Make a goal for each employee to send three cards this week.

46. **CELEBRATE EVERY ANNIVERSARY.** It's sad, but surveys show almost half of married men don't remember the date of their wedding anniversary. But just about every man can tell you the exact date he was hired by his organization. Work anniversaries are a big deal for men *and* women, so celebrate each one with the entire team. **ACTION**: Your company may only celebrate anniversaries every five years with an award, but start celebrating every work anniversary of each teammate with a quick gathering at the person's work area with a little food and sincere thanks from you.

47. **CREATE TEAM-BASED FINANCIAL REWARDS.** Says JELD-WEN's CEO Mark Beck, to build a cross-functional team it's important to have very specific objectives for each person, but also metrics, targets, and goals for the team as a whole. As for financial rewards—specifically bonuses—he believes that "You win together or die together." When Beck put this philosophy in place in one cross-functional team, his sales person balked. "He said he had no influence on manufacturing. He wanted to get paid if he got an order," said Beck. "I respected his input; but we wanted to break down the walls. He *could* actually make the plant run better. If he did a better job of forecasting with his clients, manufacturing could level-load and get costs downs. If the sales team was only paid on commission, they would never worry about something like

that." Beck said eventually that team started growing and everyone bought in. "But most importantly," he said, "it helped us all feel like a team." **ACTION**: Find a way to make one of your financial incentives (or part of a bonus) tied to overall team performance.

48. **EXPLAIN WHY.** General George S. Patton said, "Leadership is the art of getting someone else to do something you want done because he wants to do it." When you let your employees know *why* they are being asked to do something, it enables them to feel "in" on the purpose behind an action and part of the decision to move forward. **ACTION**: Think about the last request you made of an employee. Did you use have-to language? Meet with the person again and involve him/her more deeply in the decision-making process and explain the why.

49. **TELL TRUTHS AND A LIE.** An entertaining way to get to know new teammates is by playing a quick game of Two Truths and Lie. Each team member secretly writes down two truths about their work and/or personal lives and one lie. Everyone quizzes each other on their three questions. The idea is to pretend all are true. After a conversation, the group votes on which one they think is your lie. It's also a good way to find out who the poker players are. **ACTION**: In a relaxed setting this month, help team members learn more about each other by playing this or another get-to-know-you game.

50. **CELEBRATE WITH VIDEO.** To celebrate teammate Michael Andersen-Leavey's winning of the Pinnacle Award—one of the highest employee honors at 55,000 person American Express—his colleagues created a Carpool Karaoke parody

video of *Nothing's Gonna Stop Us Now* and posted it on the company intranet for all employees to see. From Manhattan to India, his fellow HR professionals drove together while singing modified lyrics to the Jefferson Starship tune—all to celebrate Andersen-Leavey's prowess at implementing new processes and policies and helping internal groups go through audits. **ACTION**: This month, celebrate an employee's above-and-beyond achievement by creating a fun video and posting it on internal or external social media.

51. **OVERCOMMUNICATE WHY.** Dan Johnson, CEO of Innovation Credit Union in Saskatchewan, Canada, says a leader must over-communicate the *why* behind business changes, and do it at least weekly in various formats. "It takes multiple touch points to communicate why we are making people go through all this disruption before they start to connect the dots," he says, "before people start saying, 'Oh, they're serious about this.'" We've found leaders get sick of their messages about mission, vision, and values long before their employees do. Typically, something important must be repeated at least five times—in various ways and over various media—before it becomes embedded. **ACTION**: Ask yourself: What do I want my employees to understand right now? How can I communicate this in five different ways over the next five weeks?

52. **IDENTIFY CAUSES OF INSOMNIA.** In a team meeting, a great question that can get people talking is "What's keeping you up at night?" Now, of course, the idea is to address business concerns, not the current political situation or unruly teenagers (you don't have enough time for those!). The most powerful part of asking this question is listening and following up,

helping your people break down barriers and overcome challenges. **ACTION**: Ask that question of your employees in your next weekly team meeting, and put together a plan—with the help of your people—to address a few of the easy fixes.

53. **GIVE BACK.** Lance Trenary, CEO of Golden Corral, told us, "It's noble to be part of something bigger than yourself. Our coworkers get excited to know they will help send nearly 4,000 kids of wounded, injured, ill, and fallen military heroes to summer camp this year (called Camp Corral), and that we donate almost $2 million a year to the DAV Charity." When a leader can articulate exactly how a team's beliefs and values come to life (such as "giving back"), those abstract ideas take on a whole new level of meaning. **ACTION**: Choose a charity to support as a team, or determine another way collectively your team can give back to your community.

54. **ESCAPE TOGETHER.** Escape rooms are a fun way to help a team understand the importance of diversity and pulling together. When Greg Piper, worldwide director of continuous improvement at Becton, Dickinson & Co., brought his global team together for the first time he took them to an escape room. "We didn't break the record but we came close," he said. "But most importantly, we all realized everybody brought something different to the team—unique talents and thinking patterns." **ACTION**: Find an outside activity to do with your team that will help them gel and recognize the importance of diversity.

55. **INVOLVE PEOPLE IN JOB REDESIGNS.** HR consulting company Morneau Shepell has researched the link between organizational change and absenteeism. The researchers had

guessed that big events—mergers, downsizings, restructurings—would have the most profound impact on employees' well-being. Instead, they discovered individual job redesign can lead to anxiety and stress even greater distress than wide-sweeping layoffs—and can be severe enough to lead to sick leave. Most leaders recognize the need for greater communication and support when making major corporate moves, but often fail to adequately support employees when changes are made that directly affect their day-to-day work lives. In contrast, we've found changes in job function can be seen as positive if the employee believes it's his choice, or at least has a voice in how the changes will occur. **ACTION**: Consider if you've changed an employee's job tasks lately. If you have, invite that person to have a discussion about how he or she can now tailor the job somewhat to fit their motivations and strengths.

56. **INVEST IN TEAMBUILDING.** At online retailer Wish, managers are given one-hundred dollars per quarter, per employee, to spend on a teambuilding activity. The money might be spent bowling together, on a dinner, for paintball, or a host of other outings. The only requirement is that the activity should bring people together beyond a work setting. Teams then use Workplace by Facebook to post photos and videos for the entire company to see. Said Ryan Giles, head of talent, "Our goal at Wish is to make shopping more fun. That's going to be next to impossible if we don't have fun with each other. These teambuilding activities have become a great way for teams to build personal relationships outside the office and inject more fun into our culture." **ACTION**: Put aside $100 per

employee this quarter and do something as a team outside of work hours.

57. **RISE AND SHINE.** A few teams we've studied regularly invite a member of the senior leadership group—from another functional area—to present to them over breakfast. Employees pepper the leader with questions about their part of the business in these Rise and Shine gatherings, and the leader tells an instructive story of how she got where she is in her career. **ACTION**: This week, invite a senior leader from a different department to come to your team for a Rise and Shine breakfast get-together.

58. **THIS STAYS HERE.** Want to get your people to pay attention in your team meetings? Use the term: "This stays in this room" and, wow, everybody perks up. Millennials especially want to be part of something bigger than themselves, so bring your people into the inner circle by providing them with information they might not normally receive: revenue numbers, competitive data, or customer trends. This kind of inclusiveness helps everyone better understand the impact their work is making to build the brand and affect the organization's performance. **ACTION**: In your next meeting, use that term and share something you might not normally have (without disclosing something you shouldn't, of course). Pay attention to the body language of your team members.

59. **ADMIT FAILURES.** When leaders are candid and transparent in their communication with teammates, people quickly learn their word means something. Your coworkers can handle the truth, the good and bad. It's clear to your people that a leader who cannot admit failure has to constantly prove himself, and

is obviously threatened by mistakes. **ACTION**: Consider: When was the last time you admitted that you made a mistake to your team? If it's been awhile, it's time to show your vulnerability this week. Admit to something (even if it's in the past) you did that missed the mark. Let people know it's okay to take smart risks and fail. That can lead to a good discussion about what a smart risk looks like in your team.

60. **CHALLENGE EACH OTHER.** There's an old saying: If two people in business always agree, one of them is unnecessary. Employees often grow up in organizations believing conflict is bad. If that's the case in your team, it's time to do some reeducation. Let people know respectful conflict on your team is encouraged. Such debate needs to be open, not behind closed doors, and focused on solving a problem versus tearing down others. Also, let your people know you want to hear everyone's voice, not just a powerful few. **ACTION**: Push your team this week to challenge each other in brainstorming and decision-making on at least one issue. You may have to appoint someone to play the role of radical to get things started.

61. **DRAFT A RALLY CRY.** In creating a team Purpose statement, the first step is to encourage input from all employees. Ask your people: "Why do we exist as a team?" or "What job do we do for customers?" or "What gets you out of bed every day?" Employees should draft their attempts independently, then the group can decide together the best language. Combine the most effective ideas into a compelling, yet brief, manifesto. **ACTION**: If you don't have a team purpose statement, meet this week and put pen to paper.

62. **START WITH YOU.** Greg Piper, a team leader with Becton,

Dickinson & Co., holds a biweekly one-on-one continuous review session (for thirty minutes) with each of his team members around the world. He starts each session with the question: "What do you want to talk about?" **ACTION**: This week, start this process by meeting in one-on-ones with your team members about their projects, goals, and tasks. What can you do to help? Start with their concerns.

63. **GIVE GREAT FEEDBACK.** An important question for new hires is: "How do you like to receive feedback?" Relevant managers explain to their people that they want to focus on their improvement and growth and, as such, will provide ongoing feedback as to how their performance is progressing, but want to deliver it in the most effective manner possible. After all, many employees hear, "I want to give you some feedback" as "I want to tear you down." Let them know that's the last thing you want. **ACTION**: Ask this question of a few of your people this week—new hires and long-tenured—and see if you are offering feedback in the best way for each individual. Then, brainstorm ways by which to improve.

64. **ROTATE LEADERSHIP.** Geese in flight rotate the lead spot frequently. Likewise, in great teams, it's not unusual for a manager to rotate the leadership position of various projects based on the work that needs to get done and the skills and motivations of the people involved. **ACTION**: Think about the next project your team has coming up. Who hasn't led in a while? Who could grow from the opportunity to lead while also providing solid guidance for the task?

65. **REACH OUT TO VIRTUALS.** There are a few rules of the road when managing a team with remote employees. First, ensure

remote people understand purpose. This means plainly elucidating not only what they and the team need to accomplish, but how, for whom, and why. Next, overcommunicate. This means speaking with each team member every day (no matter where they are in the world) via phone or a project website. Finally, it will entail listening carefully for changes in remote employees' tone or engagement levels. At these times, ask the remote employee, "What's up?" **ACTION**: Make a goal to connect with each remote employee every day for the next month, even if it's a brief connection. At the end of the month, ask your team if they think your relationship has improved, is the same, or is worse than a month ago.

66. **CREATE A FUN SQUAD.** At Ben & Jerry's, managers have long recognized the importance of making their workplace an enjoyable place to spend a day. The company has a rotating Joy Gang to plan what they call Joy Events. These have included Name-That-Face Contests, where employees bring in old photos of themselves for others to guess; to Barry Manilow Days, where the singer's birthday is honored by blasting his songs over company speakers; to Dog Days of Summer, where employees bring in their pets, who are treated to baths and all the toys and snacks they can handle. **ACTION**: Appoint a fun squad on your team with the goal of bringing a little more happiness into your workplace. Let them know that it's a six-month assignment then other employees will get the nod.

67. **GET OUT OF DODGE.** To spur the kind of creativity that leads to true innovation, we learned it's not unusual for Nike managers to take their people out of the office to put them into a

creative mindset. Teams might attend the Boston Marathon or the National Hockey League All-Star Game to see what sports fans wear; others might get a sense of what's cool in attire by hanging out at a skate park in New York City or riding the waves with the surfers at Redondo Beach. A team might also do something seemingly unrelated to sports: Some have visited movie sets while others have climbed the Sydney Harbor Bridge. **ACTION**: Break your team out of its regular routine this Friday afternoon with a field trip to someplace that might spark creativity (not a bar!).

68. **SPEAK LAST.** In the 1950s, designers unveiled the Edsel to their executive team. A curtain was drawn to reveal the prototype, and for almost a full minute the audience sat in stunned silence. Finally, according to accounts, the chairman of the board started clapping. Following him, wild applause erupted as the crowd of executives expressed their now-enthusiastic approval. Of course, consumers greeted the Edsel much the way the executive team had at first. They were underwhelmed. Firsthand accounts suggest that groupthink took hold when the well-meaning chairman began his initial burst of applause, and that shut off productive discussions about the potential albatross on the dais. The point for us: Leaders should speak last, letting others freely weigh in first. **ACTION**: Begin holding your comments until last in your team debates.

69. **FOCUS ON SELF-CARE.** More people are becoming more health conscious, yet less than half of workers in a recent poll say their companies support employee well-being and help them maintain a healthy lifestyle. Great team leaders realize that

workplace stress is one of the biggest health issues employees face, so they find ways to create healthier environments. They do things like stocking up on healthy treats for the workplace, conducting walking meetings now and then, and investing in items like stability balls or a few free weights to give people a break from sitting all day. **ACTION**: Find just one way this week to help your people be healthier.

70. **GIVE VIRTUAL TOURS.** One new virtual team we saw had members meet over desktop video and take turns giving one another quick tours of their workspaces. By panning the camera around the room slowly, they showed their remote colleagues their work environments. Some pointed out personal items, while others noted things that might distract or disrupt them such as closely seated coworkers in an open environment space, or a photocopier or water cooler nearby. After these quick tours, team members said they were better able to interpret and understand distant colleagues' attitudes and behaviors. **ACTION**: In your next meeting, have your remote employees join by video conference, and ask for a tour of their workspaces.

71. **INSTITUTE A HIRING PROCESS.** The Philadelphia 76ers employ specific criteria when hiring new sales associates. They look for passion and what they call the three C's: competitiveness, coachability, and curiosity. They also have a thirty-question personality test as part of the interview process—comparing candidates' results to those of their elite ticket-sales representatives. **ACTION**: With your team members, determine the best questions you can ask—and process to follow—to bring the right people onboard and ensure their success.

72. **DEVELOP GROUND RULES.** Toby Dodd has built successful teams in three countries for Cushman & Wakefield. His team culture centers around three guiding principles: transparency, collaboration, and diversity of opinion. But, he adds, those are just words if the leader doesn't embody them in every action. In his team in Singapore, for example, an employee was caught sending abusive letters to other workers. Within twenty-four hours, Dodd consulted HR, external and internal counsel, and terminated the individual. "Since our business was built on these principles, it was essential to show the team that this was our culture through and through. We included the leadership team in the decision, and then we talked with the whole office to answer questions and help them understand the importance of following through when our culture is compromised." **ACTION:** In your next team meeting, ask and together define, "What are our team ground rules or guiding principles?"

73. **WORK CROSS-FUNCTIONALLY.** It's been well over a hundred years since business icons Thomas Edison and Alexander Graham Bell first formed workers into permanent functional units referred to as departments—Finance, Sales, and so on. Eventually most businesses followed the lead. Along the way, some leaders started to foster rivalries between groups to encourage competition. This, they argued, brought out the best in people. While these contests may have provided some short-term gains, much more common were rivalries that developed and brought out the worst between departments. **ACTION:** Today ask your team: Are we in competition with any other teams within our own organization? If the

answer is yes, develop a plan to understand better that department's challenges and how your team and theirs might work together more collaboratively.

74. **OPEN YOUR ENVIRONMENT.** Mark Zuckerberg, CEO of Facebook, works at a communal desk shared by five other employees. He notes, "The whole idea here is that, by having an open floor plan where people work close to each other, it facilitates people sharing and communicating about what they're doing, which enables better collaboration, which we think is key to building the best services for our community." **ACTION:** Find a way to break down any physical barriers in your environment that may be preventing your people from communicating openly.

75. **INTEGRATE NEW HIRES.** Dave Checketts, one of the founding board members of JetBlue Airlines, told us that he loves Millennials. He's got a company bursting with them. And one way JetBlue integrates Millennials into the team from Day One is by inviting every single new hire—no matter where they are located—to a two-day orientation session in Florida. Young maintenance technicians rub shoulders with experienced pilots, flight attendants get to know baggage handlers. The executive team attends each orientation session, each week. The CEO provides a history of the company and details how important the culture is. This dedication to orienting people and blending generations helps each new hire immediately feel part of the team, understand the company mission (to inspire humanity), and name the five values (safety, caring, integrity, passion, and fun). **ACTION:** Put

together a formal orientation process for your new hires that will help them feel like part of the team from the first day.

76. **CREATE A TEAM INCENTIVE.** Sturm, Ruger & Co. allocates 15 percent of pretax profits every quarter to profit-sharing. Said CEO Mike Fifer, "The first year it averaged less than five percent of pay and . . . now it is more than 30 percent, and everyone is paying attention and pulling together in the same direction." This admittedly can only be implemented if you have the power to do so—if you are a CEO or small business owner, for example. But, most team leaders should be able to find a way to implement some type of collective incentive or reward. CEO Fifer said, "This sort of incentive takes a couple of years to take root in an organization. As a manager, you know it is starting to work when a junior employee takes independent initiative to save expenses or to push for higher efficiency." **ACTION**: Start a discussion today about how you could create a team incentive or reward. Is there someone you would need to involve in the planning or approval?

77. **EVALUATE THE BOSS.** At Google, employees regularly evaluate their managers. They are asked questions such as "Does your manager give you accountable feedback?" "Do you feel micromanaged by your manager?" and "Does your manager have meaningful discussions with you about career development?" Bosses who exhibit less-than-stellar results are given additional coaching, and the company says about 75 percent improve within a few months. **ACTION**: Have your team fill out anonymous 360-feedback surveys about your performance. After you've reviewed the results, let people know what

you've learned about yourself and be genuinely thankful for the feedback! Then, put a plan in place to improve where you need.

78. **EAT TOGETHER.** Dana Marlowe, principal of Accessibility Partners, said: "One way to motivate my employees is to try new restaurants. My colleagues and I are always trying out eateries that have opened up in our area. It gives us a chance to have working lunches while expanding our palates. Next week we're trying out a new Mexican place for Cinco de Mayo." The simple act of breaking bread together regularly can bring people together. **ACTION**: Every other week for the next few months, ask your entire team to lunch and try someplace new each time.

79. **PITCH & DEMO.** Anand Sanwal, cofounder and CEO of CB Insights, said his team has quarterly Pitch & Demo days where they take three days out of the office—once a quarter—to experiment with new ideas or projects suggested by team members. "Anyone can propose an idea and run with it," he said. **ACTION**: Dedicate just one day this quarter to go offsite and have your own Pitch & Demo day. Ask for employee ideas beforehand, and spend your time together improving those ideas.

80. **UNSOLICITED KINDNESS.** Recall astronaut Chris Hadfield. Each member of his crew did one unsolicited kind thing every day for every other member of the crew, and many of the acts were anonymous: One might cook a meal when it wasn't his turn, another might tidy up a sleeping area for a crewmate who had to rush to duty. These actions focused each teammate on serving others. **ACTION**: Implement this idea in your

team. You might want to make the requirement a little less arduous: Everyone does one unsolicited kind thing for every other team member once a week. Report on the results in a group meeting after a few weeks.

81. **SNAP AT EACH OTHER.** At one call center we visited, employees recognized each other for their great work not by clapping, but with finger snaps. It was 1960s poetry-reading cool. If an employee did something great, a coworker would commend them in a daily huddle and everyone would snap in appreciation. They called the recognition moments SNAPS, which stood for something meaningful to the team: Super Nifty And Positive Stuff. **ACTION:** Institute a fun ritual unique to your team to recognize employees' good work.

82. **SET UP YOUR LEADERS.** When we were in Kuwait recently, we found a terrific practice at one of the country's largest banks. If a senior executive was going to visit a branch or team, it was the branch or team manager's assignment to send a list of recent recognition winners beforehand. That way, the executive came in to the location informed about the good things that were happening, and was able to offer specific congratulations to those team members who had gone above-and-beyond. **ACTION:** Invite a senior leader to your team this week and set them up for success by letting them know of the people who have achieved something great.

83. **FIX THEIR TECHNOLOGY.** At innovation juggernaut 3M, leaders believe generating feelings of security in their teams is a basis for making creative breakthroughs. Team leadership is just as much a science as that practiced by their chemists or engineers. Leaders are expected to develop their soft skills:

To be respectful and warm with employees, keep promises, and involve their people in decision making—as well as be open and display integrity in all they do. We've found that part of creating secure environments means paying attention to the seemingly mundane, for instance, do your people have the technology they need? **ACTION**: Today, touch base with each of your people and ask if they have the tools they need to succeed, or if any equipment needs attention.

84. **REDUCE ANXIETY.** Anxiety levels for young people today are the highest observed in any generation in eighty years. Millennial stress levels are even higher than those who went to war. A friend of ours is the minister of a church congregation of young single adults all under the age of thirty. He told us his greatest contribution as the leader of this flock has been getting this generation to feel accepted, safe, and to relax. "They are so serious, so hard on themselves," he said. "If they aren't doing something amazing with their lives by twenty-five, they think they are failures." **ACTION**: This week, meet with each of your Millennial employees to help them understand their value to the team and clearly explain any steps they'd need to take to progress further in their careers.

85. **ASK WHY 5 TIMES.** At Qualtrics, a multibillion-dollar software business, CEO and founder Ryan Smith says strong teams can and should disagree. He calls this process "radical candor," which has to start with real (not fake) friendships—when teammates know their peers genuinely care about them and their success. In this kind of team, "The criticism you dole out is never gratuitous, but always in *their* best interest," Smith said. "It means that you know your colleagues

want you to succeed and that, win or lose, you're in it to-gether. With that mindset, you'll know any criticism comes from a place of encouragement because everyone is working toward the common goal of creating something great that will truly help others." **ACTION**: Instead of viewing the next argument in your team as a negative, embrace it and use the debate as a chance to improve. Ask at least five *why* questions of people who are arguing to determine the true cause of the disagreement.

86. **ADD ONE MOTIVATING TASK.** When Jane Hutcheson was vice president of learning and development for TD Bank Financial Group, she had an employee who had been at the bank for three decades. He was a solid player, but wasn't about to break any records. In a development-focused aspirational conversation, she discovered he had a passion for public speaking, but his job didn't involve giving presentations. She found an assignment for him to go into colleges to speak to groups of students about potential careers. After adding this small new task, his overall job engagement increased. We find when members of a team feel that career goals are cared about by their team leader, they usually become more ener-gized. Who wouldn't? **ACTION**: Before the end of this month, find one new assignment (even if it's small) that you could add to each person's job responsibilities that the employee would find motivating.

87. **HOW ARE YOU DOING?** One simple question asked by great lead-ers is, "How are you doing?" We know it sounds basic, but we aren't talking a quick, "How ya doin'?" as a manager passes an employee in the hall, never breaking stride. No, leaders who

are relevant to their employees' experience take the time to sit down with their people and ask with pure intent: "Really, how are you doing?" This is especially important when a leader notices a change in a person's disposition, interactions with others, or their output. The manager then listens quietly and empathetically to the answers. These chats should be face-to-face or on the phone/video conference if the person is remote, not via email, social media, or text. **ACTION**: Ask this question with sincerity of each of your people this week.

88. **HOW CAN I HELP?** The next big question great leaders ask is, "How can I help?" When managers take the time to create a supportive environment—and are willing to roll up their sleeves to help—team members eventually start to share the struggles that are going on with their projects and even in their personal lives. Leaders then build genuine relationships with their people. A boss might not be able to solve a problem with an employee's errant teenager—other than perhaps offering up a sympathetic "I'm so sorry . . . you can get through this." But the one thing they can typically do is help with work challenges. **ACTION**: Ask this question of each of your direct reports this week.

89. **HIRE BETTER REMOTES.** Mark Beck, CEO of JELD-WEN, told us that when he hires remote employees for his team, he makes sure they are driven by *autonomy*. "Some people want constant direction from the boss," he said. "Those are the wrong people to hire for your outposts. We look for those who are entrepreneurial, people who like a lot of rope." In our experience, we've also found it's important for remote employees to have interests outside of work, a way to switch

off and decompress, and to create important social connections that others may have in collaborative office environments. **ACTION**: Write down a few smart questions you might ask to improve the hiring process of remote team members.

90. **DE-STRESS.** At General Electric Canada, Sonia Boyle is vice president of human resources. She said her company found, "Stress was the number one reason for people using our employee and family assistance programs." So, GE introduced initiatives to help, including specific training for managers on how to help their employees get the support they need without fear of being stigmatized. Managers across the organization also share best practices with each other on how to create a psychologically healthy work environment, and employees across GE have volunteered to serve as "mental-health allies." They don't try to be counselors, but provide peer support to colleagues. Overall, there has been a decrease in the number of people absent from work due to psychological concerns, Boyle said. **ACTION**: Consider how you might encourage and model well-being practices in your team—giving people daily breaks, forbidding late-at-night emails, creating a more empathetic environment, and so on.

91. **PERSONALIZE RECOGNITION.** Good managers have learned to celebrate their employees' achievements, but they know awards should be personally meaningful for greatest effect. The fact is that, as a manager, the best way to know what your employees value is to ask them. That might mean changing up your reward system to incorporate days off, dress-down events, weekly team recognition gatherings, or social-media thanks. When you include things they actually want—presented in a

way they'll appreciate—team members are much more likely to put in extra effort in the future. **ACTION:** This month, have a recognition discussion with each of your people. Ask them about the best recognition moments from their career—what did they receive, how was it presented, in front of whom, and so on. Then, put together a brief recognition profile for each person.

92. **ASSIGN THREE MENTORS.** Author Bruce Tulgan is only half joking when he says a manager should prepare for an employee's first day the way a parent would for a kid's birthday party. Not that you should greet them with balloons and a clown, but you should plan in advance to *greet* them and make their first day a big day for the team. He writes about one consulting company that assigned not a single mentor on the first day, but three mentors who stuck like glue to a new hire throughout the first months—helping the new person learn how to make an impact, ensuring tasks and goals were aligned with what mattered most, and helping the new hire feel accepted and valued in the team. After a while, the employee could choose one of the three to keep as a long-term peer coach. **ACTION:** Try this with your next new hire. Assign not one, but three, mentors.

93. **ENCOURAGE DISCONNECTING.** Consulting giant McKinsey suggests that "always-on, multitasking work environments are killing productivity, dampening creativity, and making us unhappy." One of the most significant findings in employee surveys of large and small organizations is that employees have an exceptionally hard time disconnecting from work. Being always *on* is a dangerous and unproductive mindset.

Even elite athletes require time to rest and recover. **ACTION**: Be intentional about when you expect team members (and yourself) to be engaged in the office or digitally, and be intentional and explicit about when *not* to engage. Put in place a policy today about no emails after eight in the evening, or on the weekends, for example.

94. **ADD A LAUGH.** All team meetings don't have to be PowerPoint slides and yawn-inducing pie charts. Mix in a little fun with the work. In your next team meeting, insert a Dilbert comic or a lighthearted YouTube video that reinforces a point you are trying to make. At Innocent, a U.K. company, prior to one company meeting employees were asked, "What would you do with $1,000?" The question wasn't hypothetical; at the meeting the top five had five minutes to pitch their dreams to the crowd. The vote determined who got the money. We've seen other teams play Minute to Win It games at the start of their meetings: It takes 60 seconds and gets everyone involved and thinking outside the box. **ACTION**: Studies prove fun is a key factor in enhancing creativity and boosting camaraderie. Consider what you can do to add a few minutes of fun to your next team meeting.

95. **THREE GOOD THINGS.** Martin Seligman, a psychology professor at the University of Pennsylvania, developed many of the ideas used today in the field of positive psychology. He created an exercise called Three Good Things. Seligman suggested that each night, just before bedtime, people write down three good things that happened during that day—especially how they helped bring those good things about. Those positive memories are then processed during our REM sleep, and

the theory is we'll wake up more optimistic and confident. **ACTION**: Do this for two weeks and see what effect it has on your attitude at work and home.

96. **WALK AROUND**. Few things frustrate an employee more than vague statements from a boss such as: "That's not it, but I'll know it when I see it." Also clumped into this category of vague leadership are the "absentee managers," those who never seem to be available to answer questions or make a decision in a timely manner. In our research, great leaders manage by walking around. We found in the highest performing teams, managers spend an average of 75 percent of their time coaching employees one-on-one and walking the floor to ensure that their workers get the support they need to navigate the demands of their jobs. **ACTION**: This week, make it a goal to spend three-quarters of each day with your people.

97. **SHARE CREDIT**. You might recall Larry Tate from the television show *Bewitched*. Larry did a host of annoying things—like bringing uninvited clients over to Darren and Samantha's house for dinner—but what was unforgiveable was regularly taking credit for Darren's creative ideas. Back to the real world: In our surveys we've found the most frequent reason employees give for distrusting their leaders is because, "He/she took credit for my work." And most of these leaders are nowhere near as charming as Larry was. We see great leaders stand behind their teams when things are good, allowing their people to shine. And when the flack is flying, that's when great leaders move to the front and take the heat. **ACTION**: Today, gather your people and give credit where it is

due—to one of your employees for a great idea or accomplishment.

98. **BELIEVE IN THEM AGAIN.** A few years ago we met Ty, a sales rep who had been with his firm for twenty years. A new strategic-selling direction had left him floundering. Ty had gone from top ten in sales to bottom ten, and the leadership team believed that he couldn't cut it. We argued, "He can still sell, people don't lose that ability. You just have to bring it out." His sales leaders tried again. They let Ty know they cared and believed in him; they actively listened to his concerns, and they started to find ways for him to sell in this new world—playing to his strengths. Two years later, Ty was number one in the company (out of more than one-hundred sales people). **ACTION:** Do you have a long-term employee who is struggling? Today, express confidence in that person and let him/her know you'll spend more time in the coming months to help.

99. **WOW INTERNALLY.** At Boyd Auto Group, senior leaders challenged all their managers to create ten Wow experiences every day with their teams. Each manager was given ten Wow chips, and they were to start with them in their left pocket every morning. When they had a positive, reinforcing experience with a team member, they were instructed to move one of the chips from their left pocket to their right. By day's end, each of the ten chips should have moved pockets. We find that when leaders start to look more for what is going right in their workplaces, and less for what's going wrong, they reinforce a culture that can't help but translate to a positive experience for customers. **ACTION:** Try this today.

Put ten coins in your left pocket and move them to the right with each positive employee interaction.

100. **NINETY-DAY QUESTIONS.** The three-month point is important with new hires. By then, new people should feel that they are starting to fit in and making important contributions. We recommend asking these questions at the ninety-day point to gauge a person's acclimation: Is the job what you expected, and are you facing any roadblocks to hitting your goals? Are you getting all the information and training you need? What's the best thing that's happened to you so far here? Have you noticed anything we could improve upon, perhaps an idea that was effective in other places you've worked? What gets you excited about coming here to work every day, and what makes you want to hit the snooze button? This is not a performance review, it's a time to listen to people who might be still trying to find their place. **ACTION**: Ask these questions of your last new hire and listen carefully.

101. **FIND THE TIME.** During a visit to rental-car giant Avis Budget Group, we found leaders had a wonderful practice of electronically sending out a new customer service story at the start of every day about how one of their people (or teams), "Try Harder." One manager we met there took it further by sending encouraging texts at the start of every day to his people. These little notes let his team know he was cheering for them and thinking about them. It was a simple random act of kindness that meant a lot to people cleaning cars and filling out paperwork. **ACTION**: Once a week for the next month, find one great customer-service story from your team and email it to everyone.

Plus, a bonus idea:

102. **RANDOMLY RECOGNIZE.** At one professional soccer team we visited, all the employees were supposed to come to the monthly all-hands meetings thinking of someone they appreciated, someone preferably working behind the scenes who didn't get a lot of thanks. The manager would them randomly ask an employee or two whom they'd like to appreciate on the team. The person they recognized received a gift card to a local restaurant. **ACTION**: Start this practice on your team. Give your people the chance to highlight someone else and set them up for success with an award to present in each monthly meeting. You will find that all month people will be looking for the chance to make someone else's day.

ACKNOWLEDGMENTS

We owe so many people thanks for their tireless work and support in helping us launch this work. To our agent Jim Levine and his team at Levin Greenberg Rostan Literary Agency for helping us focus our message. To Emily Loose for taking our rough ideas and pushing us to make the book eminently readable and helpful. To our editor, Ben Loehnen, and the team at Simon & Schuster for your belief in this project and your support in taking it around the world. To our team at The Culture Works: Paul Yoachum, Lance Garvin, Christy Lawrence, Chris Kendrick, Dan Cook, Oz Yosri, Brody Wright, Brianna Bateman, Mark Carpenter, and our training partners including the team at Rideau: Peter Hart, Jean-Francois Grou, Jennifer Lumba, Mark Lindsay, Gord Green, John Mills, Meena Kahn, and many others. To our partner at LinkedIn Chip Cutter. To those who submitted research ideas:

Alden Durham, Glen Nelson, Anthony Gostick, and Scott Christopher.

Special appreciation to those who allowed us access into their organizations, in no particular order: At American Express: David Kasiarz, Lauren Rosenhaft, Carter Elton, and Jose Maria Zas. At the Sixers: Jake Reynolds, Scott O'Neil, Ben Cobleigh, Zack Robinson, Evan Ostrosky, Craig McClure, Michael Drobnick, Eric Cole, Braden Moore, Jill Snodgrass, and Leo Cardenas. At Ganassi: Erin Brothers and Scott Harner. At The Wendy's Company: Frank Leary, Diane Weed, and Scott Weisberg. At California Pizza Kitchen: G.J. Hart, Dave Dodson, and Kim Boerema. At JetBlue: Dave Checketts and Nancy Elder. At Tesco: Matt Davies, George Gordon, Mark Chapman, and Karl James. At Danaher Corporation: Tom Joyce, Angie Lalor, Melissa Aquino, Nicole Gavros, Danielle Rouleau, and Mark Hamberlin. At the Conference Board: Rebecca Ray and her amazing team. At Deloitte: David Dye, Sasha Rosen Brecher, Jodi Simco, and Dan Helfrich. At Fluke: Kim Cochran. At JELD-WEN: Mark Beck. At Quicken Loans: KimArie Yowell. At Bell Helicopter: Mitch Snyder, Robert Hastings, Brian Chase, Scott Drennan, Allison Hansen Mullis, and Martha Vandeveerdonk. At Skanska USA: Rich Cavallaro and Nicole Didda. At Amazon: Tanner Elton. At Applied Imaging: John Lowery. At Cushman & Wakefield: Toby Dodd. At Golden Corral: Lance Trenary and Shelli Blackwelder Buck. At Becton, Dickinson & Co.: Greg Piper. At TCC: Ryan McCarty. At Wish: Ryan Giles. At Innovation CU: Dan Johnson. At Michigan Medicine: John Charpie, Jane Pettit, Whitney Williams, Sonya Jacobs, and the MicroMentors Phyllis Blackman, Maria Ceo, Linda Grosh,

Hinke Jansen, Musty Habhab, Karen Lang, Linda Peasley, Stephanie Schroeder, Ann Smith, and Heather Wurster.

As always, we dedicate this book to those who give us their undying love and support, our families: Jennifer and Tony, and Heidi; Cassi and Braeden; Carter, Luisa, and Lucas; Brinden; and last, but not least, Garrett. These are the best teams we are blessed to be a part of.

NOTES

The people quoted in this book were interviewed by the authors unless otherwise noted below.

INTRODUCTION: SOLVING THE MODERN PROBLEMS OF TEAMWORK

1   We met Chris Hadfield when we shared the stage at the 2016 Greatness in Lethbridge Conference. Most of his comments are from that interaction, however additional material was gleaned from *Maclean's*, "The Wonder of Chris Hadfield," by Kate Lunau, May 28, 2013. And we would encourage you to learn more about Hadfield in his fascinating book *An Astronaut's Guide to Life on Earth,* (2015) Back Bay Books.

4   The 80 percent of employees' days spent working in teams is from "Collaborative Overload," *Harvard Business Review*, January–February 2016, by Rob Cross, Reb Rebele, and Adam Grant. In the same paragraph, the Deloitte survey of 7,000 executives was noted in the Schumpeter column "Team Spirit," in *The Economist*, March 19, 2016.

4   Studies showing how effective teams have a better collective intelligence, are more efficient, and happier on the job comes from *Psychology in Spain*, 2011, Vol. 15. No 1, "Work Team Effectiveness, A Review of Research from The Last Decade (1999–2009)," by Ramón Rico, Carlos María Alcover de la Hera, and Carmen Tabernero, and quotes the University of Central Florida and US Army study. The data on lower accidents and healthcare costs in that same paragraph comes from "Proof that Positive Work Cultures Are More Productive," by Emma Seppala and Kim Cameron, *Harvard Business Review*, December 1, 2015.

5   As to teams driving greater creativity and innovation for customers, as well as the diversity issue, there are several good sources for all this, including: "Creativity and The Role of the Leader," *Harvard Business Review*, October 2008, by Teresa Amabile and Mukti Khaire; and "How Diversity Makes Us Smarter," in *Scientific American*, October 1, 2014, by Katherine Phillips.

6   The 96 percent data point was quoted from the Salesforce.com September 12, 2012, blog by Nick Stein, "Is Poor Collaboration Killing Your Company?" The Deloitte/Facebook data point was from the Deloitte University Press, "The Employee Experience: Culture, Engagement, and Beyond," February 28, 2017, by Josh Bersin, Jason Flynn, Art Mazor, and Veronica Melian.

6   The best summary of the Project Aristotle work at Google was found in Charles Duhigg's article in *The New York Times*, "What Google Learned from Its Quest to Build the Perfect Team," February 25, 2016.

7   The MIT and Union College study was published in *Science* on October 29, 2010, "Evidence for a Collective Intelligence Factor in the Performance of Human Groups," by Anita Williams Woolley, Christopher Chabris, Alex Pentland, Nada Hashmi, and Thomas W. Malone.

9   Job tenure data was culled from Ryan Jenkins' website with the original source noted as Pay Scale/Millennial Branding.

9   John Chambers was quoted in "Team Spirit," *The Economist*, March 19, 2016.

10   The data point that 37 percent of workers are remote or telecommute comes from *Entrepreneur*, "6 Characteristics of Successful Remote Employees," by Anna Johansson, February 17, 2017, and is sourcing a Gallup survey of U.S. workers.

10   The 93 percent data about gig-economy employees comes from Dan Schwabel's November 1, 2016, article in *Forbes*, "10 Workplace Trends You'll See in 2017."

10   The Stanford study is from Behnam Tabrizi's paper "Cross-Functional Dysfunctional." The quote from Rick Lash and the Hay Group data is from "HR's Hard Challenge: When Employees Lack Soft Skills," by Mark Feffer, April 1, 2016, on the Society for Human Resource Management website SHRM.org. David Deming's work was quoted from "Research: Technology is Only Making Social Skills More Important," in the *Harvard Business Review*, August 26, 2015, by Nicole Torres.

10   The 2016 Hay Group survey information was from *Forbes*, "Five Key Challenges Facing Global Firms Over the Next Five Years," by Karen Higginbottom, April 22, 2015.

11   We found the source on 70 percent of office spaces being open in *Inc.* "9 Reasons that Open Space Offices Are Insanely Stupid," by Geoffrey James, February 25, 2016.

11   The assumptions about Zappos' move to Holacracy were the opinions of Jennifer Reinhold, writing for *Fortune* on March 4, 2016. Her article was entitled: "How a Radical Shift Left Zappos Reeling."

15   The data on career development being the main cause of turnover comes from the *Chicago Tribune*, "Career Development is Top Priority for Employers Seeking to Retain Talent," by Alexia Elejalde-Ruiz, March 29, 2016.

16   The Gallup 70 percent data is from "Employees Want a Lot More from Their Managers," in the *Gallup Business Journal*, by Jim Harter and Amy Adkins, April 8, 2015. The research from Stanford

University and the University of Utah in that same paragraph was quoted in "Who's the Boss," in Slate.com on October 12, 2012, written by Matthew Yglesias.

19   The story of the Caterpillar facility was found in "The DNA of Engagement" (2014) by Rebecca Ray, Patrick Hyland, David Dye, Joseph Kaplan, Adam Pressman, and the 2014 Research Fellows of The Engagement Institute at The Conference Board. The 40 percent result is from the same authors' 2015 report of the same name.

CHAPTER 1: UNDERSTAND GENERATIONS

23   Joan Kuhl was quoted in *The New York Times,* "What Happens When Millennials Run the Workplace," by Ben Widdicombe, March 19, 2016.

24   The *Time* article was the cover story on May 20, 2013, by Joel Stein, and was titled "Millennials: The Me Me Me Generation."

24   The data on the generational breaks is largely from "Here Is When Each Generation Begins and Ends, According to Facts," in *The Atlantic*, March 25, 2014, written by Philip Bump.

25   By 2020 nearly half of workers will be Millennials was from the paper "Maximizing Millennials in the Workplace," by Jessica Brack and Kip Kelly of the University of North Carolina Kenan-Flagler Business School.

26   The one-third and 66 percent statistics about Millennials are from "The 2016 Deloitte Millennial Survey."

27   The decline in homeownership rates is attributed to "Homeownership Rates Are Falling, And It's Not Just a Millennial Problem," by Shreya Agarwal, *Forbes*, May 6, 2016.

27   Data on marriage ages rising is from "5 Good Reasons to Get Married While You're Young, According To Research," by Kelsey Borresen, in the *Huffington Post*, November 14, 2013.

27   The Pew data was from, "Why 25% of Millennials Will Never Get Married," by Belinda Luscombe, September 24, 2014, in *Time*.

27   The *Time* survey about the two-year marriage model was quoted in

"The Beta Marriage: How Millennials Approach 'I Do,'" by Jessica Bennett, July 25, 2014, in *Time*.

28   Ancillary data presented on managing Millennials was gleaned from Ryan Jenkins' website and his article on that site, "A Guide to What Motivates Millennials at Work."

28   The data on sleeping with your phone comes from *Apartment Therapy*, Taryn Williford, "Why 83 Percent of Millennials Sleep with their Phones," from September 24, 2010.

29   SHRM data comes from "Generation Gap Causes Conflict in Some Workplaces, SHRM Poll Shows," posted on SHRM.org on Apr 29, 2011.

31   The quote about limited research to guide us on Millennials comes from a paper by Rodney Deyoe and Terry Fox, "Identifying Strategies to Minimize Workplace Conflict due to Generational Differences," on the Academic and Business Research Institute website.

33   The concept of cowboys and collaborators was found in the paper "Maximizing Millennials in the Workplace," by Jessica Brack and Kip Kelly of the University of North Carolina Kenan-Flagler Business School. They also made the point about younger workers wanting their managers to be mentors.

34   The terrific quote near the UNC citation (from the Millennial employee) comes from "The 8 Greatest Strengths of Generation Y," on OnlineCollege.org published on January 9, 2012.

36   The 100 positive reinforcements a minute on video games is from the positioningsystem.com blog posted September 14, 2009, "Positive and Negative Reinforcement—Oops," quoting Aubrey Daniels book *OOPS!*

40   Erin Reid was quoted from her *Harvard Business Review* article, "Why Some Men Pretend to Work 80-Hour Weeks," April 28, 2015. Marianna Virtanen is quoted from another *Harvard Business Review* article, "The Research Is Clear: Long Hours Backfire for People and for Companies," August 19, 2015, by Sarah Green Carmichael.

42 The data (14 percent) on the impact of recognition comes from the article "Recognition Programmes, Are They Important," on Deloitte.com.

49 We interviewed Harvard's Joe Badaracco and quoted him in our book *The Integrity Advantage*, Gibbs Smith (2008).

50 The information about Pope Francis was from *The Washington Post*, "Pope Francis Wants 'Absolutely Transparency' as He Pushes Vatican Reform," by David Gibson, February 12, 2015.

51 The data on Open Dining comes from "Let's Be Real: Why Transparency in Business Should be the Norm," in *Entrepreneur*, March 31, 2015, and was written by Robert Craven.

54 Bill Emerson of Quicken Loans was quoted by Bloomberg "This CEO Gives Every Employee His Cell Number (Seriously)," by Venessa Wong, November 8, 2012.

56 The 70/20/10 information comes from TrainingIndustry.com and the article, "The 70:20:10 Model for Learning and Development."

58 DreamWorks was sourced in Todd Henneman's article in *Workforce*, "Dreamwork Annimation's Cultivates a Culture of Creativity," on August 4, 2012.

59 Nietzsche's quote came from "Die Götzen-Dämmerung—Twilight of the Idols," 1895, translated by Walter Kaufmann and R. J. Hollingdale, and found on Handprint.com.

60 The information on Oprah was gleaned from *Oprah Winfrey: Global Media Leader*, USA Today Lifeline Biographies (2008), by Katherine E Krohn.

CHAPTER 2: MANAGE TO THE ONE

69 Carson Tate was quoted in her *Harvard Business Review* article, "Differing Work Styles Can Help Team Performance," April 3, 2015.

71 Sarah Perez was quoted in "The ROI of Talent Development," on the UNC Kenan-Flager Business School website, posted June 26, 2014, and written by Chad Vamos.

72 Eric Clayberg was quoted from "How Google Sold Its Engineers on Management," in the *Harvard Business Review*, December 2013, by David Garvin.

73 Waldroop and Butler are quoted from the article "Job Sculpting: The Art of Retaining Your Best People," in the September–October 1999 issue of the *Harvard Business Review*.

78 The data point that 60 to 70 percent of employers use personality assessments comes from TheGlassHammer.com and the article, "Better Leadership: Managing and Leading Different Personalities in the Workplace," by Nicki Gilmour. She is quoting Bersin by Deloitte.

88 Data and quotes on performance reviews was found in *The Washington Post* article "Study Finds that Basically Every Single Person Hates Performance Reviews," by Jena McGregor, January 27, 2014. Also from *The Wall Street Journal* article: "Human-Resources Executives Say Reviews Are Off the Mark," by Joe Light, November 7, 2010. In addition, quoted was, "The Push Against Performance Reviews" in *The New Yorker*, by Vauhini Vara, July 24, 2015; and, "Should Performance Reviews Be Fired?" on Knowledge@Wharton, April 27, 2011.

89 Richard Clark of USC was quoted from his paper: "Fostering the Work Motivation of Individuals and Teams," 2003.

90 The BetterWorks data was quoted from "Why The Annual Performance Review is Going Extinct," in *Fast Company* by Kris Duggan, October 20, 2015.

96 Susan Reilly Salgado was quoted in her *Inc.* article, "Why You Shouldn't Treat All Employees the Same," October 29, 2014.

99 We learned more about IDPs at TheBalance.com and the article "Individual Development Plan (IDP) Samples for Busy Managers," by Dan McCarthy, October 12, 2016.

102 Catherine Cole was quoted in our 2012 book *All In*.

CHAPTER 3: SPEED PRODUCTIVITY

105 The 39 percent statistic about new hires was from SHRM.org's article "Majority of New Hires Say Job is Not What They Expected," by Steve Bates, on May 28, 2013.

106 The 86 percent statistic in the next paragraph was from *Forbes*, "Why Your New Employee's First Six Months Matter Most," by Darren Dahl, May 14, 2013.

106 More onboarding data came from ActiveCollab.com and the article "A Systematic Approach to New Employee Onboarding." We also learned here about the Square and Infusion examples.

107 *The Economist* article previously cited also included the data about 73 percent of flights from NTSB.

107 Keith Rollag, et al, were quoted from *the MIT Sloan Management Review*, "Getting New Hires Up to Speed Quickly," Winter 2005, by Keith Rollag, Salvatore Parise, and Rob Cross.

109 Hylke Faber and Vijay Govindarajan were quoted from "What FDR knew about Managing Fear in Times of Change," *Harvard Business Review*, May 4, 2016.

111 We learned more about Netflix in the *Harvard Business Review* article, "How Netflix Reinvented HR" by Patty McCord, January 1, 2014.

113 Doug Soo Hoo was quoted from the *Harvard Business Review* article, "Get Immediate Value from Your New Hire," by Amy Gallo, April 15, 2010.

115 MIT's Buddy Tips comes from Welcome.mit.edu and the article "Onboarding Buddy Suggestions and Tips."

117 While researchers have not found a close match for the Antoine de Saint-Exupery quote in his works, an interesting history of the quote's derivation can be found on QuoteInvestigator.com and the article, "Teach Them to Yearn for the Vast and Endless Sea."

119 Ed Catmull of Pixar was quoted from the *Harvard Business Review* article, "How Pixar Fosters Collective Creativity," by Ed Catmull, September 2008.

121   Alex Pentland was quoted from the connection.mit.edu website and the article, "The New Science of Building Great Teams," by Alex Sandy Pentland, April 2012.

122   Information on Gallup's friendship at work can be found in the *Gallup Business Journal*, May 26, 1999, "Item 10: I Have a Best Friend at Work."

122   The 64 and 24 percent numbers come from benefitspro.com, "Work Friends Increase Engagement," by Dan Cook, September 29, 2014.

125   The TED example comes from the TEDBlog "8 Tips for Virtual Collaboration, From TED's Tech Team," by Haley Hoffman, May 4, 2015.

126   Danaher shareholder returns were noted in Bloomberg, "What Makes Danaher Corp. Such a Star," by Justin Fox, May 19, 2015.

CHAPTER 4: CHALLENGE EVERYTHING

133   The Lamborghini headline and the quote came from the *Luxury-Launches* article, March 23, 2017.

133   Amy Edmondon was quoted primarily from her March 15, 2002, paper, "Managing the Risk of Learning: Psychological Safety in Work Teams."

135   Ricardo Semler is quoted from "Managing Without Managers," from the September–October 1989 issue of *Harvard Business Review*.

138   Ray Dalio is quoted from CNBC.com, "Why Hedge Fund Titan Ray Dalio Says You Shouldn't Pull Punches When You Criticize Your Boss," by Kathryn Dill, April 29, 2017.

140   Steve Jobs was quoted from the D8 Conference 2010. His entire interview can be found on YouTube, posted September 8, 2016.

141   Geert Hofstede's work can be found on Geert-Hofstede.com.

142   We learned about *arbejdsglæde* on Whattheheckisarbejdsglæde.com.

142   Other data on Denmark came from the *Fast Company* article, "5 Simple Office Policies that Make Danish Workers Way More Happy Than Americans," by Alexander Kjerulf, April 15, 2014.

149   Linda Kaplan Thaler was interviewed and quoted in our 2008 book *The Levity Effect* (Wiley).

151 Hackman was quoted from the "Why Teams Don't Work" article in May 2009 *Harvard Business Review*.

153 Tom Kelley was quoted from *The Ten Faces of Innovation* (2005) Doubleday.

154 Jeffrey Gitomer was quoted from the foreword he wrote to our book *A Carrot a Day* (2004) Gibbs Smith.

155 Wayne Sales was interviewed and quoted in our book *The Integrity Advantage* (2003) Gibbs Smith. An article on the odometer issue was included in the *Los Angeles Times*, "Iacocca Admits Mileage Tampering Was 'Dumb': Apologizes for Chrysler's New Car 'Test-Drives' by Its Managers with Odometers Disconnected," July 2, 1987, by James Risen.

158 The Tata award was mentioned in the *Inc* article "Removing Your Organization's Fear of Failure," September 23, 2013.

CHAPTER 5: NOW, DON'T FORGET YOUR CUSTOMERS

161 Information on reef studies comes from *The Atlantic*, "Why Some Coral Reefs Are Thriving," by Ed Yong, June 15, 2016.

163 We learned about P&G's diversity work at FoxBusiness.com and the article "Why Procter & Gamble, McDonald's, and Ford are Catering to the Black Consumer," by Linda Bell, October 12, 2015. Also from TargetMarketNews.com that reposted an article by Cliff Peale, writing in the *Cincinnati Enquirer*, February 25, 2007, and his article "Procter & Gamble Advertising Targeting African-Americans has Paid Off."

164 The Kellogg study was quoted in *Kellogg Insight*, "Better Decisions Through Diversity."

164 Haas and Mortensen are quoted from "The Secrets of Great Teamwork," in *HBS*, June 2016.

165 Patty McManus was quoted from her article in *Fast Company*, July 22, 2014, "3 Types of Dysfunctional Teams and How to Fix Them."

168 Sixers' customer Derek Koss' story comes from "How Woeful Sixers

Woo the Courtside's Upper Crust," by Jane Von Bergen, April 1, 2016, on Philly.com.

169 We learned more about Ford's F-150 pickup in *Success*, "5 Inspiring Companies That Rely on Teamwork to Be Successful," by Jim Motavalli, February 16, 2016.

171 The Deloitte & Touche statistic about customer focus driving profits is from, "Customer-Centric Companies Boost Profits by 60%—and Programmatic CRM Has a Big Role," on VentureBeat.com, December 2, 2106.

174 Donald Norman was quoted from *The Design of Everyday Things* (2002) Basic Books.

179 Information on microbattles comes from James Allen's article in *The Wall Street Journal*, June 1, 2016, "The Case for Companies to Focus on Micro Battles."

180 The information on the Mayo Clinic comes from "Customer Service Can't Just be Two-by-Two: Lessons from Four Seasons to Mayo Clinic," by Micah Solomon, October 14, 2012, in *Forbes*.

181 We learned more about the MoMA project in *The New York Times*, "MoMA Will Make Thousands of Exhibition Images Available Online," September 14, 2016, by Randy Kennedy.

CONCLUSION: WHO LEFT THE GATE OPEN?

183 The information on Orban and the fall of Constantinople came from the brilliant book *1453* by Roger Crowley (2006) from Hachette Books; Crowley's September 2007 article in *Military History* Magazine; as well as *The Economist*, "The Fall of Constantinople," December 23, 1999.

TOOLKIT: 101 WAYS TO INSPIRE YOUR TEAM

192 Carrie McKeegan of Greenback was quoted from Remote.co, "Remote Work at Greenback Expat Tax Services."

192 Schwarzkopf was quoted from *The Military Leader*, "Grow Yourself . . . Grow your Team."

193 Robert Frank's research (on flow and happiness) was quoted from his *New York Times* article, "The Incalculable Value of Finding a Job You Love," July 22, 2016.

194 Garvin and Levesque are quoted from their *Harvard Business Review* article "The Multiunit Enterprise," June 2008 issue.

194 DreamWorks information was gleaned from SHRM.org, "Dream-Works Fosters Creativity, Collaboration, and Engagement," July 5, 2012, by Nancy Davis.

197 The information on Quicken Loans Incredible Concepts was from its online Great Place to Work profile.

199 Ken Blanchard's video on the DMV location can be found on You-Tube, last updated May 16, 2011.

200 The information on LevelEleven comes from the company's website and "Does Your Sales Team Celebrate the Small Wins," By Brendan Hartt.

201 Ken Segall was quoted on Fastcodesign.com, "Meetings Are a Skill You Can Master, And Steve Jobs Taught Me How," posted June 6, 2012.

201 The information on Salesforce.com comes from Staples.com and the article "Cultivate a Positive Company Culture: 5 Examples to Emulate."

202 Moz information comes from "Built, Not Bought," on Referral Candy.com

204 Wiley Cerilli was quoted in Mashable.com, "5 Startup Founders Reveal Their Best Company Culture Trips," by Dani Fankhauser, August 9, 2013.

204 LEGO information comes from the 6Q blog and the article "A Great Company Culture Example: LEGO."

207 Amy Miller was quoted in our 2008 book *The Levity Effect*.

209 Genentech information was from the company's Great Places to Work profile, as was the KPMG information.

210 The Welches are quoted from their column on Bloomberg, "Keeping Your People Pumped," September 17, 2007.

212 The data that half of men don't remember their anniversary was from, "Half of Men Don't Know the Date of Their Wedding Anniversary (And One in Four Buy Their Flowers at a Petrol Station)," in the *Daily Mail Reporter*, April 29, 2011.

215 Morneau Shepell data comes from *The Globe and Mail*, "Sudden Change in Job Functions Can Take Toll on Employees' Mental Health," by Virginia Galt, February 11, 2017.

220 Ben & Jerry's example was found on Evancharmichael.com, "Lesson #2: Remember That Happy workers are Harder Workers."

221 On the Edsel: We quote *Entrepreneur*, "3 Questions Leaders Should Ask Their Team," by Mario Moussa and Derek Newberry, August 29, 2016.

221 The data that less than half of employees believe their companies support their healthy lifestyles comes from the American Psychological Association website and the June 1, 2016, article "Workplace Well-Being Linked to Senior Leadership Support, New Survey Finds."

224 Facebook office space information and quotes come from *Business Insider*, 9/15/2015, "Mark Zuckerberg shows that he works at the same kind of desk as everybody else," by Rachel Gillett.

225 Mike Fifer of Strum, Ruger & Company was quoted in "Master Class: America's Top CEOs On The Secrets Of Motivating Employees," in *Forbes*, October 15, 2013, by Meghan Casserly.

225 We learned about Google's manager evaluation process through "Google's Quest to Build a Better Boss," by Adam Bryant on March 12, 2011, in *The New York Times*.

226 Dana Marlowe was quoted from Tech.co and the article "41 Start-ups Share How They Motivate Their Teams." Also quoted there was Anand Sanwal.

227 Information on 3M can be found on its website and the page "Respectful Workplace Principle."

228 Millennial anxiety statistics comes from Karol Markowicz's March 20, 2016, article in the *New York Post*, "'They Can't Even': Why Millennials are the 'Anxious Generation.'"

228 Ryan Smith was quoted from his *Fortune* article, "It's Time to Stop Making Fake Friendships at Work," on June 20, 2016.

229 Jane Hutcheson's story was profiled in our 2014 book *What Motivates Me* (The Culture Works).

231 Sonia Boyle of GE was quoted in *The Globe and Mail*, "Sudden Change in Job Functions Can Take Toll on Employees' Mental Health," by Virginia Galt, February 11, 2017.

232 Bruce Tulgan was quoted from his 2016 book *Not Everyone Gets a Trophy* (Jossey-Bass).

232 McKinsey was quoted from Derek Dean and Caroline Webb's article on McKinsey.com, "Recovering from Information Overload."

233 Innocent was quoted from our 2012 book *All In* (Simon & Schuster).

233 Martin Seligman's exercise we found on happierhuman.com and the article, "Three Good Things, a Small Gratitude Exercise for a Large Boost of Happiness."

ABOUT THE CULTURE WORKS

An innovator in Employee Engagement solutions, The Culture Works is home to *What Motivates Me Engagement Training* and *All In Leadership Training*, and the provider of the Motivators Assessment™—the world's most extensive scientific assessment to help individuals identify their unique blend of core motivators.

Based on decades of experience, the company's research-based training programs and *New York Times* bestselling books help managers create cultures where employees feel engaged, enabled, and energized.

To learn more, please visit **TheCultureWorks.com**.

Unlock your free resources from
The Best Team Wins

Introducing a special value for readers of *The Best Team Wins*. The following free resources are used in the *What Motivates Me Engagement Training* program and will help you, as a manager, get your team more engaged and productive.

Visit **Thecultureworks.com/bookresources** to access the following:

MOTIVATORS ASSESSMENT™—
SPECIAL DISCOUNT FOR BOOK READERS AND THEIR TEAMS

Created from the results of workplace surveys with more than 850,000 people, the Motivators Assessment™ is one of the world's most extensive and scientific assessments to help individuals identify their unique blend of core motivators.

'EMPLOYEE ENGAGEMENT SOLVED' WHITE PAPER

New 50,000-Person Research Study Unveils Findings to Unlock Workforce Potential.

With almost universal awareness about the business benefits of employee engagement, why are employees disengaging in droves?

ALL IN ENGAGEMENT NEWSLETTER

Get access to articles, our latest research, on-demand webcasts, training solutions, advice from *New York Times* bestselling authors and workplace experts Adrian Gostick and Chester Elton, and more.

AUTHOR VIDEOS

Learn from bestselling authors Gostick and Elton as they share stories from their work with highly successful teams and managers.

ABOUT THE AUTHORS

ADRIAN GOSTICK and **CHESTER ELTON** have spent two decades helping their clients build positive cultures, enhance employee engagement, and manage change. Their work is supported by research with more than 850,000 working adults, revealing the secrets behind high-performance team and organizational cultures.

They are cofounders of the training company The Culture Works and authors of the *New York Times*, #1 *USA Today*, and #1 *Wall Street Journal* bestsellers *All In*, *The Carrot Principle*, and *What Motivates Me*. Their books have been translated into thirty languages and have sold 1.5 million copies around the world.

As leadership experts, they have been called "fascinating," by *Fortune* magazine and "creative and refreshing" by *The New York Times*. They have appeared on NBC's *Today Show*, *CBS 60 Minutes*, ABC, and CNN, and have been quoted in *The Economist*, *Fast Company*, *Newsweek*, and *The Wall Street Journal*.

To learn more about Gostick and Elton, please visit **CarrotGuys.com**.